# ERUPTIONS

## AND

# EXPLOSIONS

**TRUE STORIES**

*Real Tales of Violent Outbursts*

JUDY DODGE CUMMINGS

Nomad Press
A division of Nomad Communications
10 9 8 7 6 5 4 3 2 1

This book was manufactured by CGB Printers,
North Mankato, Minnesota, United States
February 2018, Job #240587
ISBN Softcover: 978-1-61930-631-8
ISBN Hardcover: 978-1-61930-629-5

Educational Consultant, Marla Conn

Questions regarding the ordering of this book should be addressed to
Nomad Press
2456 Christian St.
White River Junction, VT 05001
www.nomadpress.net

Printed in the United States.

# Contents

# Titles in the
## **Mystery & Mayhem** Series

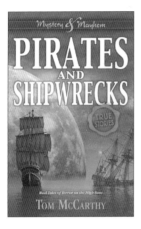

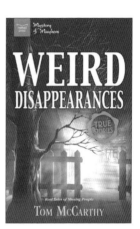

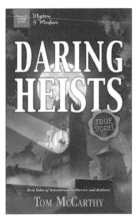

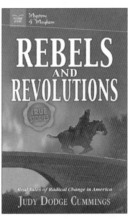

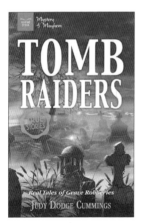

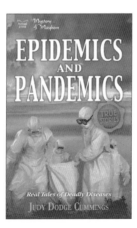

Check out more titles at www.nomadpress.net

# Rumbles and Roars
# of Earth and Man

The universe began with a bang billions of years ago as space expanded, doubling in size every fraction of a second. Since then, eruptions and explosions have never stopped rocking the planet. Some of these blowups are natural growing pains as Earth stretches her legs and cracks her knuckles.

Others are man-made, the results of technology run amuck and humans hungry for power.

The energy released when volcanoes erupt, engines combust, or bombs explode is thrilling and fascinating. It is also deadly. This book tells the stories of five violent outbursts that impacted the world long after the smoke cleared and the scattered embers cooled.

# Eruptions and Explosions

In 1815, Mount Tambora in Indonesia erupted. The blast unleashed a monstrous cloud of ash and gas into the upper atmosphere. For three years, the cloud drifted from one continent to the other, toying with the climate. Blizzards here, floods there, an occasional drought. Harvests failed and people starved as famine struck country after country.

Tambora gave the world a glimpse of the catastrophe climate change can bring.

Many explosions are caused by mankind's folly. On April 27, 1865, a steamboat full of American soldiers headed up the Mississippi River. The American Civil War had finally ended, and these men were survivors of Confederate prison camps. Skeleton-thin, sick, desperate to return to their loved ones, about 2,000 soldiers piled into the *Sultana*, a vessel built for only 300 people. In the middle of the night, an overworked boiler burst, shooting burning men into the dark waters of the Mississippi River.

The greatest maritime disaster in American history, the *Sultana* explosion is a mostly forgotten tragedy.

The bomb the United States dropped on Hiroshima, Japan, on August 6, 1945, will never be forgotten. This first use of a nuclear weapon helped end the bloodbath of World War II, but also killed tens of thousands of Japanese civilians. It introduced the world to the horrors of radiation and launched a nuclear arms race.

Nuclear energy not only fuels bombs, it also powers factories. On April 26, 1986, engineers at the Chernobyl nuclear power plant in the Soviet Union were conducting an experiment that went horribly wrong. A reactor exploded and tons of nuclear fuel and contaminated debris shot into the air. Authorities kept silent about the explosion for days as deadly radiation spread across Europe.

The area around Chernobyl will remain unfit for human life for tens of thousands of years.

The earth holds power in its core, a prize to whoever can extract it, but that prize can come with a high price. On April 20, 2010, a British Petroleum oil well in the Gulf of Mexico blew out, killing 11 people and gushing crude oil into the sea. For 87 days, experts struggled to plug the leaky well, which lay more than 5,000 feet below the water's surface. Birds and fish died. Beaches along America's Gulf Coast were closed. Fishermen went out of business and the nation struggled to find someone to blame.

The explosions and eruptions of Earth and man bring tragedy, but also opportunity. Within every story of death and destruction hides a lesson. The planet rumbles and roars, "Fix this. Stop doing that. Change your path or bad things will happen."

Read these stories and heed their warning.

Before it's too late.

INDONESIA

MOUNT
TAMBORA

INDIAN OCEAN

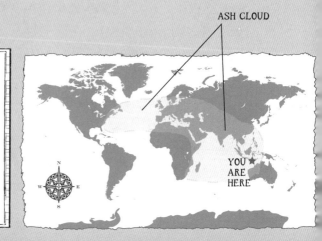

ASH CLOUD

**1815**
Mount Tambora
erupts, affecting
the climate around
the world for more
than a year. It inspires
Mary Shelley to write
Frankenstein in 1816.

YOU
ARE
HERE

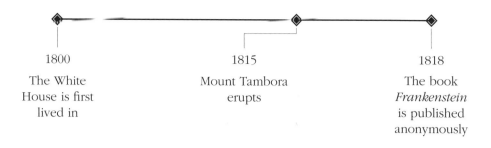

1800
The White
House is first
lived in

1815
Mount Tambora
erupts

1818
The book
*Frankenstein*
is published
anonymously

Chapter One

# Monster Awakened

In the 1818 novel *Frankenstein*, a scientist
named Victor Frankenstein toils in his
laboratory. He is trying to discover how to
bring the dead back to life. Frankenstein
stitches together scavenged body parts, injects
secret chemicals into the corpse, and on a
dark and stormy night, the creature awakens.
But something has gone horribly wrong.

Instead of a man, a monster rises from the table.

Gigantic and deformed, the hideous being has
"yellow skin [that] scarcely covered the . . . muscles
and arteries beneath." Horrified at what he has done,
the scientist flees. The monster escapes the laboratory
and tries to enter society, but everyone hates and
fears him.

FRANKENSTEIN.

*By the glimmer of the half extinguished light, I saw the dull yellow eye of the creature open; it breathed hard, and a convulsive motion agitated its limbs.
... I rushed out of the room."*

*Page 43*

*London, Published by H. Colburn and R. Bentley, 1831.*

Artwork by Theodor von Holst from the 1831 edition of *Frankenstein*

The creature is hungry for revenge against the man who abandoned him. He wanders the earth on the hunt for the scientist.

This classic tale was written by Englishwoman Mary Godwin, better known by her married name, Mary Shelley, during the stormy summer of 1816. Frankenstein's creation could have been inspired by a real-life monster— Mount Tambora. When it erupted in 1815, the volcano unleashed a powerful destructive force. Tambora's ash cloud hovered in the upper atmosphere for three years.

From there, it laid waste to the global climate.

The cloud sent snow in summer and drought in winter. Violent thunderstorms rained down on Mary Shelley's head. Did the horrors of the climate inspire her to write a horror story?

Buried in Tambora's terrors is a cautionary tale. Cataclysmic climate change has the power to kill millions of people and make life miserable for millions more.

Follow Tambora's road of ruin to understand this monster's warning to the present.

Mount Tambora is located in Sumbawa, an island on the eastern edge of the archipelago nation of Indonesia. In 1815, Tambora loomed 14,000 feet over the Java Sea, its peak jutting proudly into the sky. The small kingdom of Sanggar sat at Tambora's feet, ruled by a local leader called the raja.

April was the beginning of the dry season, a busy time on Sumbawa. The rice crop was almost ready for harvest, and village men worked hard chopping down sandalwood trees to supply shipbuilders.

Two worries kept the raja awake at night. Pirates from a northern island had preyed on coastal villages, kidnapping people to sell as slaves. And recently, the long dormant volcano on Mount Tambora had begun to rumble.

That rumble turned into a roar just before sunset on April 5, 1815. The raja thought a pirate vessel had somehow slipped to shore unseen and fired a cannon.

Then, the raja saw a flame bursting from Tambora's summit and realized the volcano had erupted. For three hours, the monster trapped inside the mountain bellowed. Then, it suddenly stopped.

The raja ordered the villagers into the rice paddies to clear the ash and dust from the plants, and he breathed a sigh of relief. The monster was slumbering once more.

But Tambora was only napping.

At 7 p.m. on April 10, the mountain awoke with a monstrous explosion. Three columns of fire burst from its peak, uniting into a massive ball of flame. The mountain's slopes glowed red as rivers of gas and rock fragments called pyroclastic flows raced to the sea at speeds of 100 miles an hour.

The air above these rivers was a searing 1,000 degrees Fahrenheit (538 degrees Celsius). As the hot air rose, cold air swept in underneath, creating a whirlwind of ash and dust. The whirlwind inhaled everything in its path and spit it back out again.

An hour later, a 15-foot-high tsunami swept inland, washing away rice fields and huts. As hot pyroclastic flows cascaded into the cool ocean, ash exploded into the air. When this ash hardened, it formed giant rafts of floating pumice. Ocean currents pushed these west.

At 10 p.m., the columns of magma shooting into the sky collapsed. A massive crater 3 miles wide and one-half mile deep was left behind. As the eruption subsided, the plains of Sumbawa began to sink.

An hour later, the whirlwind ended and the explosions began. Detonations from deep inside Tambora's belly boomed all night long. More than 1,000 miles away, local chiefs on the island of Sumatra feared they were being invaded.

Most of the 12,000 villagers who lived close to Tambora died immediately from poisoned gas, burning lava, or flying debris. Only 26 people managed to escape. These included the raja and his family, who fled inland on the only stretch of land not covered in pyroclastic flow. They made it to another village, but things were not much safer there.

All night, volcanic ash rained from the sky. This was not the soft, powdery stuff of camp fires. Volcanic ash is gritty. It's made of tiny fragments of rocks, minerals, and the glass formed when lava hardens quickly.

Villages 20 miles from the mountain were buried in ash 40 inches deep. Communities 100 miles away were covered in 10 inches of the dust. By the time Tambora stopped belching, it had ejected roughly 24 cubic miles of debris into the sky. This was enough to cover a square area of 100 miles in 12 feet of ash and pumice.

A satellite view of the summit of Mount Tambora
photo credit: NASA

Morning brought more terror. The ash cloud was now as large as Australia. The British ship *Benares* had been cruising in a nearby strait when Tambora erupted. The captain described daybreak in a world where the sun was blocked by an ash cloud blanket. "Complete darkness had covered the face of day. . . . It was impossible to see your hand when held up close to the eye."

With no sun, the air temperature plunged 20 degrees.

On the third day after the eruption, winds pushed the ash cloud away and the sun appeared again in Sumbawa. However, life did not return to normal. During the next month, many more people died.

Air thick with ash and dust caused lung problems. Desperately thirsty, people drank from wells poisoned by acidic ash. Many contracted deadly diarrhea. Crops covered in ash could not be eaten, so people starved to death, including one of the raja's daughters.

Some people resorted to eating rats or selling their own children for a cupful of rice.

Tambora killed approximately 90,000 people throughout the Indonesian islands. Sixteen years after the eruption, a Dutch official sailed along the coast of Sumbawa and reported how desolate things still looked. Tambora, he said, "has spared . . . not a single person . . . not a worm . . . not a blade of grass."

Living in England, Mary Shelley heard of the eruption of a volcano on the other side of the world. She probably did not pay much attention to the event, thinking it did not affect her. Shelley was wrong. Like a gigantic monster, Tambora had a very long reach.

When Tambora erupted, it spewed millions of tons of volcanic debris into the air. This discharge included 55 million tons of sulfur dioxide gas. The gas was hurled 20 miles into the stratosphere.

# Eruptions and Explosions

Like a monster with the power to transform, Tambora's gas combined with water vapor to form an acid mist. These liquid droplets, called aerosols, clung together in a cloud. From its perch in the stratosphere, Tambora's cloud toyed with Earth's climate long after the volcano itself had fallen silent.

People around the world noticed the sky looked different. They had no clue Tambora was the artist behind the stunning red, purple, and orange sunsets. "Sometimes storm clouds continued to glow red," one Londoner noticed, "even after the sun set."

Almost a year after the explosion, an observer in China described the sun's evening rays as "sheets of glowing pink." This was Tambora's aerosols at work.

The cloud caused sunsets the color of fire, but its impact was chilling. The aerosols reflected between 1 and 2 percent of the sun's rays, blocking this solar energy from reaching Earth. Jet streams carried the cloud toward the east at speeds of 60 miles an hour.

Within two weeks after Tambora erupted, the aerosol cloud had circumnavigated the globe, dropping a fine layer of dust along the equator. Within two months, it was causing jet streams to buckle over the Arctic. These wind currents forced cold air south into North America, Europe, and Asia and lowered the average global temperature by about 1 degree.

The volcanic winter put the world in a deep freeze.

The strange weather did not go unnoticed. Englishman Luke Howard, an amateur meteorologist who had been recording London's weather for years, noted that gales struck England almost daily in January 1816. Then, on February 9, the temperature did not get above 20 degrees Fahrenheit (-7 degrees Celsius). This was unusually chilly for the south of England.

That summer, Howard traveled to the European continent and found bizarre weather there, too. Floods were drowning towns from Amsterdam, Holland, to Geneva, Switzerland, but in Scandinavia, crops withered in the field when rain refused to fall.

Howard's records showed the average temperature in London from 1807 to 1815 was 50 degrees Fahrenheit (10 degrees Celsius). By contrast, in 1816 it was only 38 degrees Fahrenheit (3 degrees Celsius).

In 1816, Mary Shelley was in Switzerland, experiencing Tambora's wrath first hand. On June 18, she peered out the windows of the villa where she was staying with her fiancé, Percy Shelley, and some friends. Rain lashed the glass. The hilly countryside was a green blur and the waters of Lake Geneva a churning mass of gun-metal gray.

# Eruptions and Explosions

Shelley shivered and scooted her chair closer to the fire. She and her friends had been cooped up by this "almost perpetual rain" for days. Fierce winds yanked massive oaks out by their roots. Thunder split the sky, releasing sizzling spears of lightening. To entertain themselves, the friends decided to write ghost stories.

Shelley was determined to terrify her companions. She wanted to craft a story that "would speak to the mysterious fears of our nature . . . to curdle the blood and quicken . . . the heart." The wild weather fed Shelley's imagination.

The night before, she had laid in bed, unable to sleep. Suddenly, a moonbeam slipped between the cracks of her shutters and handed her a vision. "I saw the hideous phantasm of a man," Shelley recalled, and then the creature showed signs of life and stirred "with an uneasy, half-vital motion." Now, huddled close to the fire, she began to write. Out of her pen crawled Frankenstein's monster, inspired by Tambora's monstrous storms.

Europeans called 1816 the "year without summer." No summer meant no food. In Great Britain, sleet, rain, and snow during April kept farmers from their spring planting. When seed was finally sown, the chilly weather stunted it. The oat crop in England had a "yellow and unhealthy appearance."

That fall, grain harvests were 75 percent lower than usual. This limited supply led to much higher prices. In some parts of England, the price of wheat increased by 50 percent between January and May. Hungry people grew desperate and riots broke out. In May 1816, protestors in Ely, England, carried iron-spiked bludgeons and a banner that read, "Bread or Blood."

Conditions were worse on the European continent. In central Italy, it snowed so much that no wheat was planted at all. In other countries, farmers left their crops in the field late into the fall, hoping a warm spell would arrive. No such luck.

Potatoes rotted in the cold weather, and the wheat and barley did not grow enough to harvest. The price of bread soared far beyond the reach of many. Germany called 1816 the "Year of the Beggar."

Military strategist Carl von Clausewitz traveled throughout the German countryside that summer and witnessed a survival struggle. "I saw decimated people," Clausewitz reported, "barely human, prowling the fields for half-rotten potatoes."

The famine was worst in Switzerland, where Mary Shelley and her friends were trying to ward off cabin fever with scary stories. In this landlocked nation, the price of grain was two to three times higher than in countries along the coast.

# Eruptions and Explosions

The Swiss ate moss, horses, and dogs to survive. Driven to desperation, some Swiss parents abandoned their children or killed them rather than watch their sons and daughters starve.

People with money chose migration instead of murder. Russia had escaped Tambora's touch, so thousands of Swiss moved east. Others headed west for salvation. They traveled to Holland and boarded ships for the United States. The number of Europeans who immigrated to the United States in 1817 was twice that of any previous year.

Mary Shelley and her friends were wealthy. Food was expensive, but they could afford it. So Tambora did not threaten Shelley's stomach, but it did mess with her emotions, which fed the creation of Frankenstein's monster.

Her future husband, Percy Shelley, described the poor village children he encountered. They "appeared deformed and diseased. . . . Most . . . were crooked, and with enlarged throats." Mary Shelley would have seen these ragged vagabonds, too. She recreated them in Frankenstein's deformed monster, his body crooked and huge. In her story, the creature wandered from place to place, terrifying people with his ugliness and killing them with his touch.

Tambora's manipulation of the climate had created a continent full of the hungry, homeless, and sick.

———◆———

The province of Yunnan, a mountainous region in southwest China, felt Tambora's most brutal blow. Yunnan's nickname was "land of eternal spring" because all year, the temperature averaged between 50 and 71 degrees Fahrenheit (10 and 22 degrees Celsius). The moderate climate and ample sunshine made Yunnan a farmer's dream.

Until Tambora's aerosol cloud came to call.

A month after the volcano erupted, Yunnan's eternal spring ended. Rain fell in torrents, flooding fields of wheat and barley. Sprouting beans disintegrated in mud. An early frost in August nipped the rice buds.

Peasants could not afford the soaring price of food, so people filled their stomachs with a yellow soil they nicknamed, "Guanyin noodles." This soil swelled in the gut. It weakened hunger's bite, but also killed people.

China had no Mary Shelley to document Tambora's horrors with a made-up monster, but it did have Li Yuyang. This 32-year-old poet described the downpours that flooded his community in the summer of 1815.

*"The clouds like a dragon's breath on the mountains winds howl, circling and swirling"*

# Eruptions and Explosions

Li Yuyang worried about how the few grains of rice he managed to harvest would feed and clothe his family through the winter. He had reason to worry. In 1816, the weather was even worse. July snows, August rains, and September's icy fog brought famine again. Those who survived prayed that 1817 would be different.

At first, it seemed their prayers had been answered. Despite snow in western parts of the province, the wheat and bean crops ripened and villagers raced to harvest them before Tambora changed its mind. The villagers were smart to work quickly. Summer temperatures plummeted again, and frost covered the ground from June to August.

Because rice was so important to the Chinese diet, farmers had planted five different kinds, hoping at least one would survive Tambora's cruel hand. None of the five proved tougher than Tambora.

For the third summer, the temperature in Yunnan in August was three degrees below normal. Each degree shortened the growing season three weeks.

Li Yuyang documented the misery in a poem about what people do when desperate enough.

*300 copper coins for three days of life*
*Where can the poor people find such money?*
*They barter their sons and daughters on the street.*

To keep people from selling their own children for a little food, the Chinese government opened soup kitchens. They served porridge made of barley flour, broken rice seeds, buckwheat, and vegetables. It was barely edible.

Tambora gave Yunnan province one last kick in January 1818.

A heavy snowstorm destroyed the winter wheat and bean crop. The snow was accompanied by lightning, thunder, and "purple rain."

Mercifully, by the summer of 1818, Tambora's ash cloud finally cleared from the stratosphere. Eternal spring returned. That fall, farmers harvested a bumper crop.

Tambora's icy reach stretched to North America, too. On June 6, 1816, the teacher of the one-room schoolhouse in Annsville, New York, dismissed students early when it began to snow. Four children who lived 3 miles from town headed home in a group. The children, ages six to nine, were barefoot. The snowfall became so thick, the children could see only a few hundred yards ahead.

The nine-year-old boy did not panic. Instead, he concocted a plan. The younger children took turns riding on his back, their feet in his pockets.

As he trudged through the snow, the other two children ran ahead as fast as they could for as far as their frozen feet permitted. Then, the runners sat down to wait for the boy and his passenger, rubbing each other's feet to keep the blood flowing.

Using this stop-and-start method, the children walked 2 miles through snow up to their knees. Finally, a parent found the group and led them home. The nine-year-old's feet were in shreds, the handiwork of Tambora.

New Englanders labeled 1816 as "Eighteen-Hundred-and-Freeze-to-Death." Tambora turned the weather topsy-turvy. On June 5, hailstones fell on parts of North Carolina, while Boston, Massachusetts, baked at 90 degrees Fahrenheit (32 degrees Celsius). The next day brought the blizzard that almost killed the Annsville schoolchildren.

Dumping more than a foot of snow on the Northeast, Tambora destroyed the grain crop and budding fruit trees. The colorful corpses of song birds dropped from the sky.

Vermont farmers tied fleeces back on sheep they had just shorn, but many froze to death anyway.

No one used the word "famine" yet, but farmers worried that there would not be enough grain to feed their animals. Almanacs suggested turnips or potato tops be fed to livestock in the upcoming winter.

Soon, people would be eyeing those turnips and potato tops for themselves.

In July, a killing frost struck the East Coast. The second corn crop went bust. At the same time, the region suffered from a drought. In August, low temperatures finished off any surviving corn, along with the potatoes, cucumbers, and pumpkins.

A Maine reporter wrote, "What is to become of this country . . . this part of the [nation] is going to suffer for bread and everything else." The growing season that summer in New England was shorter than average by an astounding 55 days.

Many New Englanders decided to try their luck elsewhere, in the fertile valleys between the Ohio and Mississippi Rivers. Grain was growing in the Midwest just fine, and, thanks to Tambora, global demand was high. Entire communities of New Englanders loaded up their wagons and headed west. In 1816 alone, 42,000 people migrated to Indiana.

Very few people actually had the money to buy land in the west. They needed to borrow it. To fuel the land rush, the National Bank issued 22 million dollars' worth of credit to small community banks, which in turn granted loans to settlers heading west.

The entire enterprise was a gamble that depended on the weather.

# Eruptions and Explosions

The settlers borrowed money based on their confidence that farming would be profitable. The banks issued loans based on the same confidence. It was a risky investment built on hope for a future that had not yet arrived.

In July 1818, the National Bank got cold feet, deciding the gamble was too risky. It sharply reduced the credit available to settlers and increased the interest rate on loans.

The economy might have been able to handle this single blow, but it was quickly followed by another one. Tambora's ash cloud washed out of the stratosphere. Normal weather returned, and in the fall of 1818, European farmers harvested a bumper crop.

All those New England farmers who moved west to plant grain now had no buyers.

A bushel of Pennsylvania wheat worth $3.11 in 1817 could be bought for 82 cents in 1821. These farmers had no cash with which to repay their loans.

A full-blown financial crisis struck the United States. Farmers went bankrupt. Banks ran out of money. Farms were abandoned. A volcano on the other side of the world had caused the very first economic depression in the United States.

# Monster Awakened

Like Frankenstein's monster, Tambora was large and loud and terrifying. But unlike the fictional character, Tambora was not man-made. Mother Nature gave the world Tambora. In exchange for its destruction, the volcano offered a warning.

The global climate is again undergoing a transformation. As temperatures warm and glaciers shrink, sea levels rise. Storms grow more violent and heat waves more intense. No mega volcano is causing these changes—humans are.

The food people consume, how and where they travel, and the waste they produce all emit gases that trap heat in the atmosphere. Climate change is happening again, but this time we don't have a volcano to blame.

The Intergovernmental Panel on Climate Change predicts the global temperature will rise between 2.5 and 10 degrees in the next century.

Tambora impacted the climate for three years and killed millions of people. How many people will die if human-induced climate change is not brought under control? Tambora was the monster that manipulated the climate of the early nineteenth century. The human race is the Frankenstein of the present. Humans created this climate change monster and only they can destroy it. Heed Tambora's warning, before the current monster wakes up.

TENNESSEE

GEORGI

MEMPHIS

SITE OF
DISASTER

MISSISSIPPI RIVER

MISSISSIPPI

ANDERSONVIL
PRISON
CAMP

LOUISIANA

VICKSBURG

GULF OF MEXICO

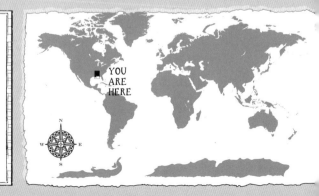

### April 27, 1865
The steamboat *Sultana*
is overloaded with freed
prisoners of war on
their way home. The
boiler explodes in the
night, burning and
drowning nearly
2,000 people.

YOU
ARE
HERE

N
W        E
S

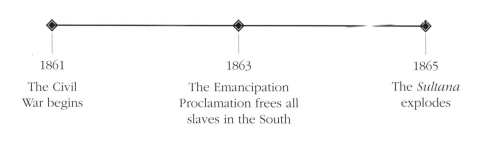

1861
The Civil
War begins

1863
The Emancipation
Proclamation frees all
slaves in the South

1865
The *Sultana*
explodes

Chapter Two

# The Forgotten Tragedy

The deck of the steamboat *Sultana* rocked and
groaned as more and more war-weary Union
soldiers climbed aboard. They shoved and
squeezed and pressed up against each other,
each person trying to carve out some space. Men
sat on the roof of the pilothouse, leaned over
the guardrails, and squeezed beside the boilers
that occupied the center of the main deck.

No one wanted to be left behind in Vicksburg,
Mississippi. These soldiers had survived the
battlefields of the Civil War and the brutality of the
Confederacy's prison camps. Now, the *Sultana* was
finally going to take the men home.

Most of them never made it. On April 27, 1865, the
*Sultana* exploded in the greatest maritime disaster
in United States history. It was a tragedy caused by
mechanical malfunction and human greed.

# Eruptions and Explosions

The fateful meeting between the soldiers and the *Sultana* was set in motion four years earlier. On April 12, 1861, the United States erupted in civil war over slavery. Eleven Southern states broke away from the country and formed the Confederate States of America, a new nation where whites had unrestricted ownership of African American slaves. But President Abraham Lincoln claimed such a move was illegal.

Battle lines were drawn. The Southern army was called the Confederates, or Rebels, and the Northern army was the Union, or the Yanks.

What everyone assumed would be a short conflict ended up dragging on year after bloody year. At first, the Union and Confederacy exchanged men captured in battle. But by 1863, prisoners of war were held in large camps. Some of these were more dangerous than the battlefield.

Captain J. Walter Elliot of Company F of the 44th Regiment of United States Colored Troops was one such prisoner. An Indiana man, Elliot was captured by the Confederates near Nashville, Tennessee, on December 2, 1864. He was transported to what Elliot called "that hell of hells," Andersonville.

The Andersonville prisoner-of-war camp in Georgia covered 27 acres. Built to house only 10,000 men, by the time Captain Elliot arrived, 33,000 Union prisoners were packed into the camp. Most men slept outdoors, covered by a thin blanket or nothing at all.

photo credit: John L. Ransom

Food and water were in short supply. On good days, the prisoners received a 2-inch square of cornbread, a cup of beans, and a bit of bacon. When meat ran low, several men shared a pig jaw, usually one that was slightly rotten.

One sluggish stream that trickled through the camp was used for both drinking water and bathing. Diseases such as typhoid and dysentery from drinking contaminated water killed thousands.

In such an environment, the smallest scratch became infected. Medical care was so bad that a rumor persisted among the prisoners that the Confederate doctors were actually executioners in disguise. Captain Elliot said the prisoners were left with, "The bitter, bitter feeling that our country had abandoned us to our fate."

Finally, the day Captain Elliot had been waiting for arrived. On March 20, 1865, an order rang out across the prison camp. "Get ready for exchange." No bands played and no crowds cheered as the prisoners filed out of camp.

All the men were thin and grimy. Their scaly skin and threadbare clothes crawled with vermin. Every gaunt face told a story of misery, but now they were going home.

Or so they thought.

———◆———

After traveling by train, steamer, and foot, the prisoners from Andersonville finally reached Vicksburg, Mississippi, on March 26, 1865. The men were taken to Camp Fisk, a parole camp about four miles outside the city. When they saw the American flag hanging over the camp, the prisoners wept. This was their first glimpse of the stars and stripes since being captured.

Camp officials took the men to the warehouse where supplies were stored, called the commissary. Moved by the sight of these walking skeletons, the officials insisted the prisoners "take something." Captain Elliot and some other men rolled out "barrel after barrel of pickled cabbage."

They marched around and around the barrel, dipping their hands in and "ravenously devouring the cabbage and licking vinegar from our fingers." Camp Fisk was the prisoners' temporary home while they waited for Union and Confederate officials to finalize the exchange of prisoners.

On April 9, Confederate General Robert E. Lee surrendered his army to Union General Ulysses S. Grant. The war was almost over. Word came through the Confederate communication lines that the prisoners at Camp Fisk could be exchanged for Rebel prisoners held in the North. Union officials were ordered to keep track of every soldier sent home so the exchange would be even.

By this time, more than 5,000 Union prisoners of war had arrived at Camp Fisk. Many were sick. All were desperate to get home. The military was under a lot of pressure to move these men north as quickly as possible.

To speed up the process, the Army created a sweet deal for private steamboat captains. The government would pay $5 for every enlisted man and $10 for every officer that a steamboat captain transported north. Suddenly, there was big money to be made in Vicksburg, Mississippi.

The situation was ripe for corruption.

———————◆———————

## Eruptions and Explosions

J. Cass Mason, the captain and part-owner of the *Sultana*, was broke in April 1865. Earlier in the war, the government had confiscated one of his steamboats when officials caught him hauling supplies for the Confederates. To recoup his losses, Mason poured every last cent into the *Sultana*. He was banking on the two-year-old steamboat to get him out of debt.

The *Sultana* was a state-of-the-art vessel. It looked like a tiered wedding cake.

The main deck was the closest to the water. It held the ship's four boilers and the engine. Above that was the deck with the passenger cabins and saloons. The third full deck was the hurricane deck, on which stood two tall smokestacks. In the center of the hurricane was the texas, a small narrow cabin that housed the crew. Atop the texas was the pilothouse.

The *Sultana*, 1865
photo credit: Library of Congress

From the pilothouse, the steamboat pilot steered the boat around curves and obstacles in the river. Powered by steam, two huge paddle wheels, one on each side of the boat, churned through the water.

What made the *Sultana* special were its four boilers. Tubular boilers, a recent invention, generated more steam than the old-fashioned boilers, so less coal was used. This saved money. The box of each boiler was 18 feet long and 46 inches across, each one filled with steam and boiling water. Under the boilers was the furnace, in which coal burned constantly to keep up the steam pressure inside the boilers.

The metalwork around the furnace, the furnace itself, and the boilers were red-hot.

Even though the *Sultana* was only two years old, its tubular boilers were showing wear. That was Captain Mason's fault. Earlier that spring, he had raced from New Orleans, Louisiana, to St. Louis, Missouri, in only four days and seven hours, the fastest time of the season. Mason won a pair of elk antlers as his prize, which he proudly displayed between the smokestacks on the hurricane deck. This victory came with a cost, however.

The key with the *Sultana*'s tubular system was not to let the boilers get too hot. Small tubes that ran from each boiler box to the ship's chimney released smoke and gas so the pressure inside the box did not rise too high.

River water circulated around the tubes constantly, drawing heat from the metal and turning it into steam. This water level had to be monitored. Even the slightest dip in the circulating water caused the inside walls of the boiler box to overheat.

On the speedy trip that had earned a set of elk antlers, the *Sultana*'s boilers took a beating. The steam pressure rose higher and higher as the boat raced faster and faster, its paddle wheels churning through the muddy Mississippi. Every time the water level inside the box dropped too low, hot spots developed on the metal walls.

No change could be seen from outside the boiler.

———◆———

Captain Mason and the *Sultana* left St. Louis on April 13 to make their way back down to New Orleans with passengers and cargo. The Mississippi River was swollen from spring rains and the current ran fast. Two days into the journey, the crew heard stunning news at a stopover in Illinois.

President Abraham Lincoln was dead, shot in the back of the head by an assassin. The nation was in an uproar as people grieved Lincoln and a manhunt began for his murderer.

The *Sultana* reached Vicksburg on April 16 and then, Captain Mason received good news.

Thousands of Union soldiers were at Camp Fisk waiting for a ride home, and Uncle Sam was paying steamboat captains to take them. Captain Mason felt he deserved some of this pot of gold. But he still had to take his passengers and cargo to New Orleans. What if other steamboats loaded up the soldiers before he returned to Vicksburg?

Captain Mason needed someone to rig the situation for him. Colonel Reuben Hatch was just the kind of man Mason was looking for.

Colonel Hatch had served as a quartermaster throughout the war, an official who keeps the army supplied with food, fuel, and material. As a quartermaster, Colonel Hatch handled large sums of money. He also found ways of slipping some of this cash into his own pockets.

At the start of the war in 1861, Colonel Hatch had been quartermaster in Illinois. There, he was investigated for overcharging the government for lumber and bribing lumber companies so he could get a kickback from government contracts he steered their way. When investigators demanded Colonel Hatch's accounting books, he threw the books in the Ohio River to destroy evidence of his crimes. Investigators fished the records out before they were ruined.

Colonel Hatch might have been convicted, but he had connections. His brother, Ozias Hatch, was a personal friend of President Lincoln.

# Eruptions and Explosions

Strings were pulled and a committee of civilians handpicked by Lincoln reviewed Colonel Hatch's case. The committee found him innocent of any wrongdoing and Colonel Hatch was returned to active duty. His brother called in a few more favors and, by 1864, Colonel Hatch was chief quartermaster for the Department of Mississippi. So he was present at Vicksburg when the *Sultana* made a stop on its journey south.

The exact deal Captain Mason and Colonel Hatch worked out on the Vicksburg wharf is not known, but it was something like this. Colonel Hatch promised that when Captain Mason returned from New Orleans, there would be enough soldiers to fill the *Sultana*. In return, Captain Mason pledged to give Colonel Hatch a kickback, a portion of the money he would receive for transporting the soldiers north.

What Captain Mason and Colonel Hatch were doing was illegal. But they may have justified their behavior. Who were they hurting, after all? The soldiers would get home and that's what mattered.

The *Sultana* left New Orleans on April 21 with 250 passengers and 10 crew members, including chief engineer Nathan Wintringer. When the boat was still hours south of Vicksburg, Wintringer discovered steam leaking from a thin crack in one of the boilers.

The leak was serious. The engineer told Captain Mason the boat must be repaired in Vicksburg.

For the rest of the journey, Wintringer lowered the steam pressure inside the boilers. This also lowered the *Sultana*'s speed, which did not make Captain Mason happy. Would Colonel Hatch keep his end of the deal and have a load of soldiers waiting at Vicksburg or would they already be gone by the time the *Sultana* limped into town?

◆

The top commander of the Department of Mississippi, Major General Napoleon Dana, wanted to speed up the process of moving the former prisoners of war north. It was a matter of life and death. It was a matter of life and death to soldiers such as Epenetus McIntosh. This private from Illinois had weighed 175 pounds when he was captured in Georgia in 1864. Months in a Confederate prison camp had shrunk him to 80 pounds by April 1865.

General Dana put Captain Frederick Speed in charge of organizing groups of prisoners and getting them on available steamboats.

Two steamboats were loaded and headed north on April 22 and 23 without difficulty. This reduced the number of prisoners at Camp Fisk to about 2,500. The *Sultana* arrived in Vicksburg the night of April 23. Captain Mason was anxious to get a large load of soldiers on board before another steamboat arrived, but the boat's boiler needed attention first.

A local boilermaker named R.G. Taylor was brought on board to inspect the crack. "Why didn't you repair the boiler at New Orleans?" he asked.

"It wasn't leaking then," Wintringer said.

"I need this patched as quickly as possible," Captain Mason insisted.

"Two metal sheets must be replaced," Taylor replied. "Not just patched. It's for the safety of yourselves and your passengers."

"I don't have time," Mason insisted. "Just patch it."

Taylor shook his head. "If you don't let me repair this boiler the way it needs repairing, I won't have anything more to do with the *Sultana*." He walked off the steamboat.

Wintringer followed him. What words changed the boilermaker's mind are not known. But Taylor agreed to patch the leak. It took 20 hours. Still, Taylor thought all four of *Sultana*'s boilers looked damaged and did not think the boat was safe.

No one seemed to share the boilermaker's concern.

Meanwhile, Captain Mason was trying to fill his steamboat with soldiers. Captain Speed was trying to process soldiers properly, with a careful roll call.

He wanted to keep track of which men were headed to which state and what steamboat they would be sent on. This took time. The night of April 23, only 400 soldiers were cleared to sail on the *Sultana*. Captain Mason was livid. This was not the deal he had worked out with Hatch.

Mason went up the ladder to Brigadier General Smith. He agreed with Captain Mason that since the *Sultana* had been contracted by the War Department to transport soldiers, Captain Mason should get his soldiers.

"The rolls do not have to be prepared in advance," Brigadier General Smith assured Captain Mason. "It can be done on board the *Sultana* as easily as it can be done at Camp Fisk."

The decision was made. The next day, all the prisoners would go home on the *Sultana*. General Dana asked Captain Speed the total number of soldiers currently housed at Camp Fisk. Speed replied, "Between 1,300 and 1,400."

Speed had undercounted by 1,000 men.

The morning of April 24, the *Sultana's* boiler was still being patched when the first trainload of soldiers from Camp Fisk pulled into Vicksburg and filed down to the dock.

# Eruptions and Explosions

As the soldiers climbed on board, they could hear the boilermaker hammering on the ship's boilers. If there was an explosion, one soldier said, they would all "go higher than a kite." Little did this man realize he was forecasting the future.

The *Sultana*'s legal carrying capacity was only 376 people. By the time the first trainload of soldiers had been loaded, there were 968 passengers on board.

"Isn't this too many men for this boat?" asked Captain Kearns.

"The *Sultana* can handle it," a crew member replied.

But there were many more soldiers to come. The second train from Camp Fisk arrived with 400 prisoners at 2 p.m. A mixup by Camp Fisk officials resulted in none of these soldiers being counted as they boarded the *Sultana*.

An hour later, the steamer *Pauline Carroll* tied up at the wharf right beside the *Sultana*. Captain Kearns was relieved. The *Sultana* was full and there were still more soldiers coming from Camp Fisk.

"The *Pauline Carroll* is going upriver empty," he told Colonel Hatch. "Should this steamer take a portion of the prisoners?"

Colonel Hatch telegrammed Captain Speed out at Camp Fisk. "Is there more prisoners than can go on the *Sultana*?" he asked. "The *Pauline Carroll* has arrived. Shall I detain her?"

Captain Speed said no. The *Sultana* could take them all. But Captain Speed was not on the wharf so he did realize how crowded the *Sultana* was. Colonel Hatch did, but for every soldier loaded on the *Sultana*, he got a kickback from Captain Mason.

Hatch gave Kearns a pointed look. "Do not detain the *Pauline Carroll*."

The third and final train out of Camp Fisk arrived in Vicksburg in the evening. Captain Speed personally accompanied this train to the riverfront and now he realized his prisoner count had been off. These men from the last train had trouble finding room on the packed vessel. The topmost deck was so overloaded, it began to sag.

An officer complained to Captain Mason that the steamboat was too crowded. The soldiers felt like they had been "packed in like hogs more than men."

"I can't help it," Captain Mason replied. "All of you must go on the *Sultana*." He failed to mention the fee he was collecting for each man on board.

Captain Speed told Captain Mason he feared the boat was overloaded, but the captain assured him, "the men would go through comfortably and safely."

Captain Kearns reluctantly told the captain of the *Pauline Carroll* that the War Department did not need its services. That steamboat left Vicksburg with 17 people.

# Eruptions and Explosions

No one knows exactly how many people were on the *Sultana*. Records from Camp Fisk show the facility was holding 2,146 prisoners. The steamboat also carried civilian passengers, guards, and crew.

Historians estimate more than 2,500 people boarded the *Sultana* for this fateful trip. The boat also carried 250 hogsheads of sugar weighing 1,200 pounds each, 97 cases of wine, 100 mules and horses, 100 hogs, and an alligator in a wooden crate.

At 9 p.m. on April 24, the *Sultana* departed Vicksburg. For many it would be their last journey.

The night air was cool and a light drizzle fell, but the men's spirits were not dampened. The healthier soldiers sang and danced and talked about "the many good things we would have to eat" when they reached home. A group of Kentucky soldiers snuggled up next to the boilers to stay warm.

But there was also much suffering on board the *Sultana*. The diarrhea, scurvy, and malnutrition caused by months in Andersonville had not vanished during their short stay at Camp Fisk. Grown men weighed less than 100 pounds.

Men stretched out on every inch of the decks and roofs, some with no blankets. The soldiers had just hard bread and salt pork to eat.

The *Sultana* had only one cooking stove and this was reserved for the civilian passengers and crew.

The crew's biggest concern was that the *Sultana* might capsize because of how overcrowded it was. Only 10 hours into the journey, this almost happened. When the *Sultana* stopped briefly at Helena, Arkansas, a photographer on the river's bank prepared to take a picture. Word spread among the men. The soldiers swarmed to the port side of the boat and the vessel tilted dangerously to one side.

Captain Elliot was sitting on the roof of the pilothouse at the time. "Be careful!" he yelled. "Move to the other side." Expecting the boat to tip over any second, he grabbed hold of a life preserver.

The boat stabilized and the photographer snapped the picture. It was the last photograph of many of the *Sultana*'s passengers.

This was not the last time the *Sultana* threatened to capsize, however. Every time the steamer passed another vessel or an interesting sight on shore, the soldiers crowded to one side. The ship tilted, draining the cooling water away from the high boilers, which quickly overheated.

When the boat stabilized, water rushed back into the overheated boilers again, hitting the red-hot tubes and turning into steam. The pressure inside the boilers grew, pushing against the patched metal.

# Eruptions and Explosions

———◇———

The evening of April 26, the *Sultana* docked at Memphis, Tennessee, and passengers found out that the U.S. Cavalry had killed John Wilkes Booth, President Lincoln's assassin. Around 11 p.m., the boat steamed on to Hopefield, Arkansas, to pick up coal.

As the passengers bedded down for the night, Captain Mason moved anxiously about the ship. No longer did he feel the calm certainty that the *Sultana* was invincible. He confided to one passenger that he would give up his shares of the steamer if only "it was safely landed in Cairo, Illinois."

Soon, the only sounds were the snores of the soldiers, the rush of water through the paddle wheels, and the steady exhaust from the boat's engines. The pilot manned the wheel from the pilothouse at the top of the steamer. The second engineer watched over the boilers on the main deck. Captain Elliot was in a cot in a cabin on the boiler deck. He fell asleep around midnight, dreaming about how soon he would see his family again.

At 2 in the morning, the *Sultana* was 7 miles out of Memphis, approaching a bend in the river. Without warning, three boilers erupted simultaneously. With the fury of a volcano, the explosion drove fragments of the metal boilers, pipes, bricks, timber, and machinery through the upper decks. The entire center of the *Sultana* ripped apart.

The detonation rocked the countryside. People asleep inside their homes on the Tennessee shore reported a sound like "a hundred earthquakes."

Captain Elliot bolted upright, his "face, throat, and lungs burning as if immersed in a boiling cauldron." He groped his way between the cots and out the stateroom door. Suddenly, the floor disappeared and Elliot caught himself just before he fell into a gaping hole at his feet. He look down and saw "mangled, scalded human forms heaped and piled among the burning debris on the lower deck."

Chunks of the upper decks, including most of the pilothouse, had been blown away. The *Sultana*'s pilot had fallen into the wreckage below.

Passengers woke to find themselves hurling through the air over the river. Others never woke at all. When the boilers exploded, a geyser of steam and boiling water shot into the night and rained down on top of people. Some were burned to death instantly, while others were blinded. Pieces of the boat became as deadly as any weapons the soldiers had faced on the battlefield. One soldier was impaled by a piece of wood.

People pushed past Captain Elliot, panic driving all reason from their minds. Some threw themselves over the guardrail into the river. Others searched desperately for anything to help them float. Tables, doors, and pieces of wood were tossed overboard and men jumped in after them.

One soldier remembered the crate the *Sultana's* alligator was kept in. He found the creature in a closet and stabbed it to death with his bayonet. The man tossed the carcass aside, threw the crate overboard, jumped in after it, and used it for a raft. The soldier was rescued three miles downriver, still floating on the alligator crate.

Captain Elliot was frantically trying to decide if he should take his chances on the boat and burn to death or jump in the river and drown.

"Captain, will you please help me?"

Captain Elliot turned at the voice. A bruised and scalded man, covered in wreckage, sat on a cot. Both his ankles were broken, the bones breaking through the skin. The man had fashioned a tourniquet from his suspenders to stop the bleeding from his legs.

"I can't swim," Captain Elliot said.

"Throw me in the river, is all I ask," the man pleaded. "I'll burn to death here."

Captain Elliot and another soldier lifted the injured man as gently as they could and tossed him over the guardrail. It was not murder, but mercy.

Captain Elliot found one of the few life jackets and was just putting it on when a woman rushed past him toward the guardrail. He grabbed her and put the life jacket around her neck.

It was the honorable thing to do, but now Captain Elliot was done for. "I had no chance to escape," he said, "and death seemed inevitable."

But the river was not going to get him without a fight. Captain Elliot threw a mattress overboard and jumped. As he fell through the air, four men in the water seized the mattress and they all went under— with the mattress.

Down, down, down in the icy water went Captain Elliot. A drowning man clutched at his legs. Captain Elliot kicked him off and pushed himself toward the surface. When he reached it, Captain Elliot gulped a huge breath of air, but his throat burned as though he was swallowing fire.

Suddenly, the mattress was there in front of him and only one man clung to it. Elliot latched on to the sodden bed. The *Sultana* loomed above him, its burning wheelhouse poised to fall. Elliot and the other man kicked frantically to get out of the way. The wheelhouse crashed into the river, barely missing them.

The two men struggled to stay afloat in a sea of desperate people. Some floated on the carcasses of dead horses, some on live ones. People clung to debris from the wreck, boxes, bales of hay, and drifting logs. Captain Elliot and the other man on the mattress floated out of the crowd until they were alone on the dark river.

# Eruptions and Explosions

They drifted about five miles before hitting a sand bar. The icy water had numbed Captain Elliot's body so badly he could not sit up. He knew if he did not get moving, he would die. Elliot rubbed and pinched his arms and legs, harder and harder. Finally, he warmed up enough so he could stand on the sand bar.

The other man, dressed only in his underwear, was not moving. Captain Elliot whipped the man with a thin tree branch. The fellow moaned and begged Captain Elliot to stop. Captain Elliot felt guilty, but he kept hitting to get the man's blood circulating.

The torture did the trick. The man crawled on the sand bar and managed to stand up. Other people floated by, and Captain Elliot pulled a woman and two men out of the water. All three died quickly, their bodies too cold to recover.

Captain Elliot and the other man paced the sand bar. Minutes seemed like hours. The only sounds were the splash of the water against the sand bar and the gurgles of a dying man hanging onto a tree a short distance from them. This same scene played out up and down the river.

People who survived the blast now clung to life.

Time was running out. These soldiers were diseased and malnourished. The chilly embrace of the river was draining away their body heat. Scores of men died during that night.

Dawn came slowly, as if reluctant to shine light on the horrible sights. Elliot looked around him. The man who had gurgled in the night lay entangled in branches nearby, lifeless eyes staring at the sky. Half-frozen soldiers sat in trees along the riverbank. The roof of one of the *Sultana*'s cabins held six soldiers.

Another man clung to a bare tree trunk that protruded from the river. Desperate to reach a fork in the tree where he could rest, the man tried to pull himself up, but he kept slipping. Each time, he fell further down. Soon, only the man's chin was above water. Captain Elliot wished he could swim out and rescue the man.

Then, a Confederate soldier from the Arkansas side of the river pushed a boat into the water. The Civil War was not officially over. This rebel was the enemy, but he did not act like it. The rebel rowed to the tree and dragged the almost lifeless Yankee into his boat. He rowed the man to the cabin roof where the other soldiers rubbed the man's limbs until his blood warmed.

Eventually, a steamer from Memphis appeared. The Confederate soldier ferried each survivor from that stretch of the river to the steamboat. Captain Elliot was the last person rescued by that rebel. Elliot called his savior "my chivalrous knight of the gray," referring to the gray of the Confederate Army uniforms.

◆

The charred skeleton of the *Sultana* sank at 9 in the morning on April 27. By noon that same day, the last rescue boat docked at Memphis. A total of 786 people with burns, cuts, broken limbs, and hypothermia from the cold river survived the explosion of the *Sultana*. At least 200 of them died shortly afterward.

Bodies pulled from the water were laid side by side along the riverbank so friends and relatives could search for loved ones. The dead continued to wash up until the middle of May, some as far as 120 miles away. The hull of the *Sultana* had sunk in water 26 feet deep. A few burned bones and blackened skulls were retrieved from the wreck, but many people, including Captain Cass Mason, were never found.

Who would be held responsible for this disaster?

Three military commissions investigated the explosion on the *Sultana*, but they did not agree on the cause. Was it the leaky boiler? The overloaded boat? A flaw in the tubular boiler system?

The only official to face a court-martial was Captain Frederick Speed. He was found guilty of neglect of duty for putting too many men on the boat, but the verdict was overturned. An army judge concluded the *Sultana* had been overcrowded, but not overloaded.

No one knows exactly how many people were killed when the *Sultana* exploded. The total number of dead could be as high as 1,800. Whatever caused the explosion, there is no denying that human greed killed people on the *Sultana*. The boat might have exploded with only 1,000 men on board, but fewer people would have died.

No one was ever held accountable for the tragedy.

The *Sultana* explosion is the United States' greatest maritime disaster, but few Americans today have ever heard of it. Bad timing doomed the event to the dustbins of history. There was a lot going on in April 1865. General Lee surrendered to General Grant on April 9. President Lincoln was shot on the 14th and died on April 15. On April 26, John Wilkes Booth, Lincoln's assassin, was killed by U.S. troops.

In the predawn hours of April 27, the *Sultana* exploded on a quiet stretch of river far from the big cities and newspapers of the East Coast. No presidents or generals were killed on the *Sultana*. The men who died were farmers and clerks and bricklayers. After four years of war, Americans were tired of tragedy. The South was busy licking its wounds and the North wanted to celebrate peace. So the *Sultana* explosion sank deep into the recesses of the national memory.

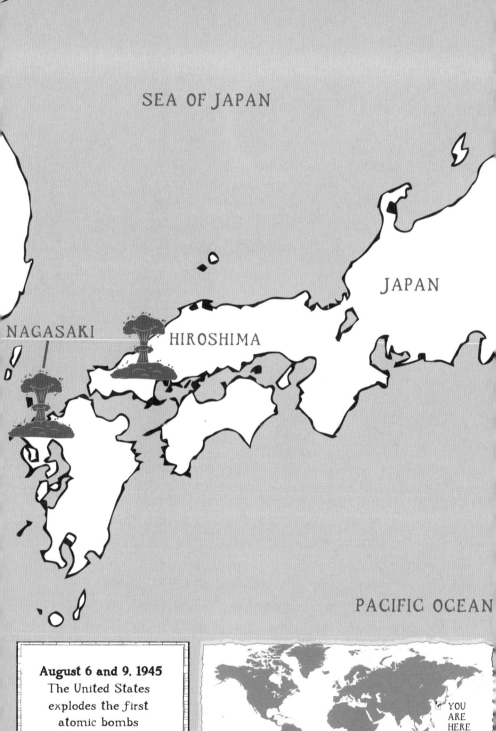

SEA OF JAPAN

JAPAN

NAGASAKI     HIROSHIMA

PACIFIC OCEAN

**August 6 and 9, 1945**
The United States
explodes the first
atomic bombs
over Hiroshima and
Nagasaki, Japan, killing
tens of thousands of
Japanese civilians.

YOU
ARE
HERE

| | | |
|---|---|---|
| 1939 | 1941 | 1945 |
| World War II begins | The Japanese attack Pearl Harbor and the United States enters the war | The United States drops atomic bombs on Hiroshima and Nagasaki, Japan |

Chapter Three

# Countdown

In Hiroshima, Japan, on the morning of
August 6, 1945, 13-year-old Yoko Moriwaki
rose early. She traveled by ferry, train,
and foot to the center of the city—she
had a day of hard work ahead of her.

Japan had been at war with the United States since
1941. By 1945, Japan was losing the fight. Short
of manpower, the government ordered teenagers
to help the war effort by tilling fields, working in
factories, digging bomb shelters, and clearing debris.
Yoko loved her country and wanted to help. On
August 5, 1945, she wrote in her diary, "Tomorrow, I
am going to clear away some houses that have been
demolished. I will work hard and do my best."

By 7 a.m., Yoko and more than 200 girls from
her school were assembled at the Koamicho Tram
Station. They formed two lines and began passing
tiles and bricks to each other.

# Eruptions and Explosions

At 8:15, a single plane flew overhead. Its silver belly opened and a bomb called Little Boy dropped out of the hatch. The countdown to Yoko's death began.

Little Boy was a powerful new weapon—an atomic bomb. Such a deadly device had never been used on people before. No one knew just what it would do. U.S. President Harry Truman chose to drop this bomb on Japan to force the country to surrender.

———◆———

The path to Hiroshima's destruction began many years earlier. During the 1930s, fascist governments emerged in Germany, Italy, and Japan. Fascism is a type of government that encourages extreme patriotism. Children are taught at a young age to worship the nation more than anything else, even their own survival. In fascist countries, no one can vote, the government controls the economy, and there is no freedom of speech or the press.

In Germany, Adolf Hitler and the Nazi Party gained political control with help from a brutal secret police. Then, Hitler wooed the German public, promising to make Germany great again. The army swelled and weapons factories churned out guns and tanks.

European leaders stood by as Hitler gained control of Austria and Czechoslovakia.

But when Germany launched a surprise invasion of Poland on September 1, 1939, Great Britain and France drew the line. Europe erupted into World War II, fought between the Axis powers and the Allies.

Germany and Italy were leaders of the Axis Powers, while Great Britain and France initially led the Allies. The Soviet Union joined the Allies after it was invaded by Germany in 1941. The United States remained neutral.

On the other side of the world, Japan had also built up military might in order to conquer an empire. Since its founding 2,500 years earlier, Japan had been ruled by the same dynasty. Emperor Hirohito was the 124th leader in this family line. He was both the head of the government and the head of Shinto, the main religion of Japan. Hirohito was honored by the Japanese people, but he did not wield much power.

The prime minister and cabinet held the real power in the Japanese government. Most of these men were fascist warlords who wanted Japan to control as much area as possible. Emperor Hirohito gave his opinion only when the cabinet was deeply divided.

Through tight control of the press and the education system, these warlords revived an ancient Japanese belief that the emperor was part god. If the citizens believed their ruler was a god, they would do anything for him.

# Eruptions and Explosions

Since the emperor followed the cabinet's orders, the warlords had total power over the country.

As a small island nation, Japan depended on imports to survive. The warlords craved territory rich in coal, iron, and oil so they wouldn't have to rely on other countries for these products. They expanded Japan's army and ordered shipyards to crank out aircraft carriers, battleships, and destroyers. Then, the army marched, seizing Manchuria in 1931 and invading China in 1937.

Franklin Roosevelt, president of the United States at the time, worried about Japan's domination of Asia, especially when Japan formed a military alliance with Germany and Italy in 1940. When Japan invaded Indochina in 1941, Roosevelt cut off all trade with Japan, including in oil. This was a major problem for the Japanese military machine, which depended on this oil.

The Japanese warlords decided to launch a surprise attack against the United States to destroy the U.S. Pacific Fleet. America would be powerless to block Japanese expansion across the Pacific Ocean.

Japan's attack was a terrible shock. At 7:55 a.m. on December 7, 1941, Japanese planes filled the sky over the U.S. naval base of Pearl Harbor in Hawaii. In two hours, 20 ships and more than 300 aircraft were crippled or destroyed and 2,403 Americans were killed.

photo credit: U.S. Navy

American neutrality ended. The nation plunged into a two-front war, with Germany and Italy in Europe and Japan in Asia.

War breeds invention. When World War II began, military scientists looked for weapons in the smallest place possible—inside atoms.

Everything in the universe is made up of atoms. These tiny particles are millions of times smaller than a human hair. Inside each atom is a dense core called the nucleus and inside the nucleus are even smaller particles called protons and neutrons. Whizzing around in the space outside the nucleus are electrons.

Atoms contain a strange energy. They can be split when a neutron breaks out of its nucleus and shoots into the nucleus of another atom. In 1939, Austrian physicist Lise Meitner developed the theory of nuclear fission. Meitner believed that when the nucleus of an atom is split, it launches a chain reaction that creates energy. The atom's neutrons fire into the nuclei of neighboring atoms. These atoms in turn shoot off their own neutrons. This chain reaction would go on as long as there were atoms to split.

The result would be a gigantic explosion.

Jewish scientists were terrified at the thought of Germany making a weapon with "atomic energy." German leader Adolf Hitler had steadily and brutally persecuted Jewish people since taking power in 1933. Leo Szilard, Edward Teller, and Albert Einstein, Jewish physicists who had escaped Europe before World War II began, wrote to President Roosevelt in the fall of 1939. They urged him to take "quick action" to develop an atomic bomb before Germany could.

Roosevelt paid attention. He authorized a top-secret bomb development program called the Manhattan Project. Army engineer General Leslie Richard Groves headed the project and chose physicist J. Robert Oppenheimer to oversee the scientific side of things. About 150,000 people at different sites around the country worked on developing an atomic bomb.

Most of them had no clue what they were working on.

General Groves' philosophy was simple: "Each man should know everything he needed to know to do his job and nothing else." Husbands could not tell their wives what they worked on. Words such as "bomb" and "uranium" were banned. Building and testing sites were referred to by code names. The bomb testing laboratory was in the New Mexico desert.

———◆———

By 1945, the United States was beating Japan, but the cost of victory was high. On April 1, 1945, 200,000 troops landed on Okinawa, an island on the southern tip of Japan. The battle for this 60-mile chunk of land took three months and killed more than 12,000 Americans. Japanese troops chose death over surrender.

The battle for Okinawa sent a clear message to Washington, DC. An invasion of mainland Japan would be deadly for American soldiers.

While the sands of Okinawa were turning red with blood, Yoko Moriwaki was starting high school. On the first day, Yoko was made deputy captain of Class 6. Her father had been away fighting in the war since 1944, and on April 6, Yoko noted in her diary, "If Father were here, he would have been overjoyed."

# Eruptions and Explosions

So far, no bombs had fallen on Hiroshima. For months, dozens of other Japanese cities had been bombarded by American B-29 airplanes. On March 9, hundreds of American planes dropped almost half a million canisters of napalm on Tokyo. This jellied petroleum exploded into flames on impact, killing more than 100,000 people in one night. Residents of Hiroshima felt lucky they had been spared.

But the U.S. military was saving Hiroshima for later. To demonstrate the weapon's huge power, military officials wanted to strike an undamaged city.

On April 12, Yoko's school had a bomb drill. That night, she wrote in her diary that the most important thing to remember during an evacuation "was to be swift and silent." Yoko had 116 days left to live.

That same day, Harry Truman wrote a friend that "the world fell in on me." On April 12, President Roosevelt unexpectedly dropped dead of a brain hemorrhage and Vice President Harry Truman took over as president. The responsibility of defeating Germany and Japan now fell on his shoulders.

Secretary of War Henry Stimson told Truman that very soon, the United States would have "the most terrible weapon ever known in human history." One bomb capable of destroying an entire city.

# Countdown

———◆———

Truman declared May 8, 1945, as V-E Day—Victory in Europe. After six long years, Germany had finally surrendered. Americans danced in the streets, but their fighting was not over.

While Americans celebrated the end of war in Europe, a ceremony was held across Japan to remember the day the country declared war on America. At Yoko's school, the war proclamation was read out loud and a special ceremony was held to honor soldiers. The Japanese government wanted to fire up citizens' patriotism. They would need to defend their homeland when America invaded.

Yoko was ready. In her diary entry for June 5, she wrote, "Whatever it takes, we must work as hard as we can until we win the war." She had 90 days left to live.

By then, it was clear that Japan would lose the war. The Japanese "Big Six" met to figure out what to do. The group of military and political leaders was officially called the Supreme Council for Direction of War. Three men were hardliners who believed every Japanese man, woman, and child should fight to the death rather than surrender. The other three men were moderates looking for a way to end the war without destroying the country.

The hardliners won the debate. Japan would fight on.

Behind the scenes, Emperor Hirohito sought a route to peace. He directed one of the moderates, Foreign Minister Shigenori Togo, to ask the Soviet Union, which had not declared war on Japan, to mediate a peace treaty between Japan and the United States.

Throughout May and June of 1945, Togo sent frantic appeals to Soviet diplomats. The United States had cracked Japanese communication codes, so President Truman knew Japan wanted to surrender. But Japan wanted to surrender on its own terms.

The United States had no intentions of letting the Japanese government call the shots. Truman insisted Japan simply give up—an unconditional surrender.

———◆———

On July 16, Yoko learned how to make a triangular bandage to wrap an injured head, ears, eyes, and chin. Soon, neither bandages nor history would matter to Yoko. She had 21 days left to live.

The day Yoko learned to fold bandages, a drama unfolded in New Mexico. The bomb-testing team assembled its first complete atomic bomb. It was called "Trinity." Scientists took refuge in bunkers miles away from where the bomb perched on the top of a steel tower in a remote part of the desert.

A warning siren sounded and the observers lay on their bellies with their faces pressed to the floor. At 5:29 a.m., the first atomic bomb in history exploded.

In a millionth of a second, the nuclear chain reaction was sparked. Radiation waves shot out of the bomb at the speed of light. A fireball as brilliant as the sun rose above the earth. The cloud swelled like the head of a jellyfish, reaching 40,000 feet high. It turned from orange to purple as it expanded.

A shock wave broke with a sharp crack, followed by a roar. The cloud belched ash and debris across the land. Men 10 miles away were knocked to the ground. In a 2-mile radius, all life was destroyed.

When the explosion settled, the scientists rose to their feet and looked at Trinity's destruction. A few people applauded and others wept. The steel tower on which Trinity had sat had been vaporized. One scientist congratulated General Groves. "The war is over."

"Yes," Groves replied. "After we drop two bombs on Japan."

President Truman had other options. American troops could invade Japan. Truman rejected this. It put too many American lives in danger.

American pilots could continue the B-29 bombing raids. This option was also discarded. By the summer of 1945, 66 cities had been demolished by American bombers and still the Japanese fought.

Some scientists urged the president to demonstrate the bomb's power by dropping it on a deserted island while international observers watched. This option was tossed out, too. What if the bomb was a dud?

Truman decided the only way to convince Japanese leaders to give up was to bomb a large, undamaged city. In his memoirs, Truman wrote, "I regarded the bomb as a military weapon and never had any doubt that it should be used."

President Truman was in Potsdam, Germany, meeting with British Prime Minister Winston Churchill and Soviet Premier Joseph Stalin when he got word that Trinity had successfully exploded. These leaders were hashing out plans for the post-war world.

Truman had come to the conference determined to convince Stalin to declare war on Japan. If the United States had to invade mainland Japan, Truman wanted Soviet help. But Truman did not trust Stalin. The Soviet Union was not a democracy, and U.S. officials feared if the Soviet Army moved into Asia, it would never leave. The news about Trinity gave Truman hope that he could end the war without Stalin's help.

On July 25, General Groves wrote up the official bombing order. Depending on weather conditions, the first atomic bomb would be dropped on Japan no sooner than August 3. Additional bombs would be delivered as soon as they were ready. Four cities were listed as potential targets: Kokura, Niigata, Nagasaki, and Hiroshima.

On July 26, Truman and Churchill issued the Potsdam Declaration, which laid out the terms for Japan's surrender.

- The power of leaders who had started the war must end "for all time"

- Japan's military must disarm

- Japanese war criminals would be tried by the Allies

- Allied forces would occupy the country until Japan had a democratic government

The declaration ended with a final warning. Japan must accept these conditions immediately or face "prompt and utter destruction."

When Japan's Supreme Council read the Potsdam Declaration, members were horrified. They believed signing it would be the same thing as signing Emperor Hirohito's death warrant. The council decided the country would fight on.

Yoko did not know Japan's leaders had received a final ultimatum from the United States.

# Eruptions and Explosions

The day the Potsdam Declaration was issued, she wrote in her diary about how happy she was that her older brother, Khoji, had moved back home: "Things will be quite lively at home from now on." She had 11 days to live.

In the predawn hours of August 6, the crew of *Enola Gay* took off from Tinian Island in the Pacific Ocean and headed for Japan. In the belly of the B-29 they carried the atomic bomb called Little Boy.

At 7:50 a.m., pilot Lieutenant Colonel Paul Tibbets said, "We're about to start the bomb run."

The crew put on their flak jackets and slipped on their goggles. The bombardier put his eye to the bombsite and spotted the target, a bridge in the center of the city.

At 8:15, an alarm sounded. The plane's bomb hatch opened and Little Boy plunged toward the earth. The crew began the final countdown to detonation.

When it was 1,900 feet over Hiroshima, Little Boy exploded. The flash was soundless. For a millionth of a second, the core of the fireball was a temperature of 1 million degrees Fahrenheit (555,538 degrees Celsius). Radiation saturated the city.

In a one-third-mile radius, every living thing transformed to ash and bone. The ground temperature was between 5,400 and 7,200 degrees Fahrenheit (2,982 and 3,982 degrees Celsius). Water in tanks and ponds boiled. Trees exploded and tile melted.

A cloud that was every color of the rainbow rose 45,000 feet into the sky. A rolling brown mass spread over Hiroshima. The tail gunner on the *Enola Gay* described the scene below. "It's like bubbling molasses down there . . . fires are springing up everywhere . . . it's like a peep into hell."

The shock wave from the explosion rippled through the city at speeds of more than 270 miles per hour. This nuclear wind slammed down brick buildings and punched out windows. Every brick and wooden structure in a 1-mile radius was obliterated and concrete structures were badly damaged.

Tens of thousands of people in a 1½-mile radius of the bomb blast were decapitated, disemboweled, crushed, and blasted with radiation. The drop in air pressure ruptured peoples' eardrums and blew their eyeballs from their sockets.

People who died instantly were the lucky ones.

Pockets of fire urged on by the strong wind united into a firestorm. Trapped under wreckage, people who had survived the blast burned to death.

# Eruptions and Explosions

The heatwave dehydrated people. Extreme thirst hurt more than their wounds. "Mizu!" The people of Hiroshima cried. "Water."

Crowds gathered around puddles and ponds. Some people dove into water tanks only to be boiled alive. The river became an oasis of death. People crawled to its bank, drank their fill, and then fell in and died.

Yoko and her schoolmates had been working a half mile from the bomb blast. Most were killed instantly. Yoko had been facing away from the blast so her face was unharmed, but her back, legs, and hands were charred. On hands and knees, Yoko headed for home. She crawled for hours until a military truck picked her up and took her to a village where a school had been turned into a relief center.

photo credit: U.S. Army

A local woman named Hatsue Ueda tended Yoko at the school. She draped a light kimono over the girl's naked and burned body. She fanned her and dripped green tea into Yoko's mouth. Ueda had no medical training, but she knew Yoko would not survive so she just tried to ease the girl's pain.

Yoko pleaded for her mother. A doctor called Yoko's home, but no one answered. Hour after hour, Yoko lay in agony, her eyes glued to the clock. "Isn't Mother here yet?" she asked again and again.

"She'll be here soon," Ueda replied. "Be strong and stay with me, okay?"

Yoko's mother never came.

At 11:24 p.m., the doctor checked Yoko's pulse. Her heart beat slower and slower and then it stopped. Yoko Moriwaki died on August 6, 1945. She was 13 years old.

President Truman got word that Little Boy had exploded as planned while he was traveling by ship back to the United States. The president released a bulletin over the radio in which he warned the Japanese government that if it did not accept America's surrender terms, the country could expect "a rain of ruin from the air, the like of which has never been seen on this earth."

# Eruptions and Explosions

But in Japan, no news came out of Hiroshima. All communication lines had been destroyed in the explosion. Hardliners in the Supreme Council viewed Hiroshima as just one more bombed city. Its destruction would not convince them to surrender, but something else would.

On August 8, the Soviet Union declared war on Japan. More than 1.5 million troops slammed into the Japanese army along the Soviet border with Japanese-occupied Manchuria.

This invasion frightened the Supreme Council more than the atomic bomb. With the Soviets as the enemy, no one was left to help Japan negotiate better surrender terms from the United States. Also, the Soviet Army would be ruthless. The Soviets had lost a war to Japan in 1905 and were still bitter about it.

On August 9, the Supreme Council met in a bomb shelter under the Imperial Palace in Tokyo to decide what to do. Three hours into the meeting, a messenger arrived. The Americans had dropped another "special bomb" on the city of Nagasaki. More than 39,000 people had been killed instantly.

Just before midnight, the Big Six decided to ask Emperor Hirohito to break their tie. He joined the men in the bomb shelter. The moderates said the nation should agree to all America's demands except one. Emperor Hirohito must remain as Japan's leader.

The war minister disagreed. "We should live up to our cause even if our 100 million people have to die. . . ."

Emperor Hirohito listened silently to everyone. Around 2 a.m., Prime Minister Suzuki bowed to the emperor and asked him to decide. Should Japan surrender or fight to the last man?

Hirohito spoke quietly. "Japan should surrender unconditionally," except the emperor must be allowed to remain. The time had come "to bear the unbearable, in order to save the people from disaster. . . ."

The Truman administration received word that Japan was willing to surrender on the morning of August 10. Now it was America's turn to debate.

The United States had insisted on unconditional surrender and the Japanese had given in on everything but the emperor. Should the United States let Hirohito stay or continue to fight? Truman's advisers came up with a compromise. The emperor could remain, but with no military power.

This requirement was telegrammed to Tokyo, and the Supreme Council resumed its debate. Hardliners argued that the United States was trying to make Japan a slave nation.

# Eruptions and Explosions

The moderates said the Americans were offering "a dim hope in the dark." While they argued, the war continued.

Between August 10 and 14, 1,000 more B-29s bombed Japan. Another 15,000 civilians died. Another six Japanese cities were added to the list of potential targets. Atomic bomb assembly lines kept running.

The Big Six once again turned to the emperor. The morning of August 14, they met with Hirohito again in the palace's bomb shelter. Hirohito listened to each man and then he said, "It is impossible for us to continue the war anymore. I would like to save my people's lives even at my expense."

Later that day, the Japanese government issued a statement. The emperor accepted the terms of the Potsdam Declaration. World War II was finally over.

Hiroshima was a graveyard. For weeks, survivors fished bodies from the river, pulled corpses from under debris, and hauled the dead off by wheelbarrows. Bodies were burned in huge piles, filling the air with the stench of death from morning to night.

The death toll from the single bomb was huge.

Little Boy killed 78,000 and wounded 37,000. Of the city's 90,000 buildings, 55,000 were destroyed, including schools, hospitals, theaters, banks, and the phone company. The military and industrial plants on the edge of Hiroshima were undamaged.

In the weeks following the explosion, uninjured people became ill. Their gums bled. Their hair fell out. Exhaustion, fever, and diarrhea plagued them. Small blood spots appeared on their skin and death followed soon after.

These people were also victims of Little Boy. The atomic bomb was radioactive. This poison contaminated the wreckage that rescuers dug into, the water they drank, and the food they ate in the days after the bomb fell. Victims of the radioactive fallout from the bomb almost doubled Hiroshima's death toll by the end of 1945.

On August 6, Yoko Moriwaki had left her diary at home. She died that day, but her words survived. These words tell a tale too often left out of history, the experience of a young girl trying to survive in a war zone while in the world around her, leaders argued, weapons exploded, and armies clashed. Yoko's life and death document victory's terrible price.

LATVIA

RUSSIA

LITHUANIA

● MINSK

BELARUS

● WARSAW

POLAND

CHERNOBYL

● KIEV

UKRAINE

ROMANIA

**April 26, 1986**
The Chernobyl
Nuclear Power Plant
suffers a nuclear
accident that sparks
the displacement of
hundreds of thousands
of people.

YOU
ARE
HERE

RADIATION
RANGE

N
W E
S

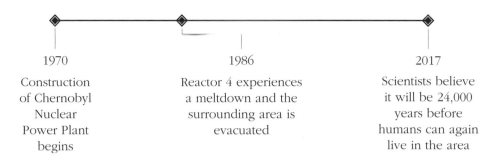

| 1970 | 1986 | 2017 |
|------|------|------|
| Construction of Chernobyl Nuclear Power Plant begins | Reactor 4 experiences a meltdown and the surrounding area is evacuated | Scientists believe it will be 24,000 years before humans can again live in the area |

Chapter Four

# The Ghosts of Chernobyl

Today, the city of Pripyat in northern Ukraine is home only to ghosts. The Cultural Palace stands empty, its rooms full of dust and debris. Trees push up through cracks in the sidewalk and moss grows on empty streets. A Ferris wheel stands in the center of a public square, empty seats groaning in the breeze.

The residents of Pripyat fled more than 30 years ago, after a reactor exploded at the Chernobyl Nuclear Power Plant just a few miles away. The reactor had a design flaw, but it was human error that transformed Pripyat from a city of life and laughter to a poisoned land unfit for humans for tens of thousands of years.

# Eruptions and Explosions

———◆———

From 1922 to 1991, the Soviet Union, now called Russia, was a country made up of 15 republics. It stretched across Eastern Europe and into Asia.

The Soviet Union was born out of a communist revolution in 1917. Communism is a system of government in which the state owns all land and businesses and is supposed to control these for everyone's benefit. In the ideal communist society, no one would be rich or poor. The nation's wealth would be shared equally.

Equality was the dream of the communist revolution, but not the reality that developed in the Soviet Union.

To get anywhere in life, a person had to join the Communist Party. Members got better jobs, higher salaries, and cars, houses, and vacations that nonmembers could only imagine. Party leaders controlled where Soviet citizens lived, what jobs they performed, what was taught in school, and what was printed in the newspaper.

Party members stubbornly clung to the belief that communism was a perfect system. If something went wrong in society, officials quickly covered it up. Anyone who criticized the government was considered a traitor, and a secret police force called the KGB would come for them one dark night.

In this secretive, fearful society, people did not share information. Weaknesses were disguised and mistakes covered up.

This culture of secrecy contributed to Pripyat's tragic fate in 1986.

About 50 miles north of the city of Kiev, in the republic of Ukraine, the small town of Chernobyl was surrounded by forests. The Pripyat River ran lazily through miles of marshland.

In the late 1960s, Soviet leaders decided this was the ideal spot to build a nuclear power station. They believed nuclear power was the key to Soviet economic growth. Construction on the Chernobyl Nuclear Power Plant began in 1970.

The project took a long time. First, tens of thousands of workers from across the country were hired. To give them a place to live, the city of Pripyat was built from scratch. Constructing the power plant took longer. Blueprints were not delivered on time or not at all. Parts were scarce, so engineers cobbled together their own.

Finally, in the fall of 1977, Chernobyl's nuclear reactor 1 was up and running. The electrical power it generated saved the country 3½ million tons of coal per year, and reactors 2 and 3 soon followed.

Soviet philosophy was, "the bigger the better," so construction began on reactor 4. Party officials pressured the project director to complete the unit early, offering huge bonuses if the job was done by the end of 1983.

But getting electricity from nuclear power is not as simple as flipping a light switch.

◆

In the early twentieth century, scientists discovered that splitting the nucleus of an atom could release energy. This process is called nuclear fission. In 1954, the Soviet Union became the first country to feed nuclear-generated electricity into the power grid.

The type of reactor used in the Chernobyl plant was the RBMK. This model used an element called enriched uranium 235 as fuel to heat water. The hot water created steam. The steam propelled turbines. The turbines created electricity.

The core of the nuclear reactor was a huge graphite block built like a honeycomb with 1,600 fuel channels running through it. Tubes filled with uranium pellets were housed in these channels. Uranium is a radioactive element with huge energy potential.

But radiation rays can also kill, so the power inside the reactor had to be controlled.

That was the purpose of the other channels in the honeycomb. Control rods could be lowered into the reactor's core through these channels. These rods absorbed the neutrons in the uranium, slowing down or stopping the rate of fission.

By the time reactor 4 was ready for approval, several small accidents had occurred at other nuclear plants with RBMK reactors. Soviet leaders knew the model was flawed. However, they kept these accidents secret, not just from the public, but also from engineers at other power facilities, including Chernobyl.

The final safety check that needed to be performed on reactor 4 involved testing what would happen if the plant lost power unexpectedly. But 1983 was almost over and everyone wanted their bonus.

Officials postponed the test, the reactor was approved, and bonuses were paid.

The view of Chernobyl from Pripyat
photo credit: Jason Minshull

Reactor 4 went on line on March 27, 1984, and the news was splashed across the front page of newspapers. Party officials posed proudly for photographs to show the world how technologically advanced communism was. Construction began on two more reactors.

Soon, Chernobyl would be the largest nuclear power plant in the world.

◆

Sasha Yuvchenko was in a good mood the evening of April 25, 1986. The day had been so unseasonably warm that the 24-year-old engineer took his toddler for a bike ride. That evening, for no reason other than his good mood, Yuvchenko dressed in a suit before he headed to the Chernobyl power station for his night shift.

When Yuvchenko clocked in at midnight, he was surprised to learn that the safety test scheduled for that day had been delayed until the night shift. But that was okay. The test should be easy. Yuvchenko later said, "I was thinking that I wouldn't have much to do that night." He was very wrong.

Inside the control room of reactor 4, Deputy Chief Engineer Anatoli Dyatlov was in a bad mood. He had been at the plant all day preparing for the safety test, only for outside officials to order him to postpone it until after midnight. Now, he was tired and cranky.

Dyatlov was admired for his engineering knowledge, but feared even when he had had a full night's sleep. He was aloof and demanding and no one liked to cross him.

Also working in the control room was shift foreman Alexander Akimov and three young and inexperienced engineers who were eager to learn from this test. It was the first time they had powered down and restarted reactor 4.

The reactor usually operated at 1,700 megawatts of power. To perform the safety test, engineers had to slowly lower it to 700 megawatts. The safety manual said the power should never go lower than 700, because the RBMK was unstable at low power.

Manning the reactor's controls was 26-year-old engineer Leonid Toptunov. As he slowly lowered the power level, a digital gauge showed the power fall to 500 megawatts. He tried to raise it, but the power plunged down to 30 megawatts. Alarms blared.

Dyatlov was furious. "What have you done, you idiot? You've let the power drop too far."

He ordered Toptunov to remove all of the control rods from the reactor's core. This would speed up the nuclear fission inside the reactor and increase power again, but it was also like cocking a gun.

Control rods serve as both the gas and the brakes.

# Eruptions and Explosions

Below the heavy lid of the reactor, the uranium filled fuel rods were releasing enormous heat. The control rods absorbed some neutrons and controlled the speed of this process. With all the rods removed, Toptunov would not have any ability to slow down the fission process.

Toptunov hesitated. "Shouldn't we shut down the reactor first?"

Dyatlov yanked him away from the control panel, ordering another engineer to take his place. The message was clear. No one refuses to obey an order from the top engineer. The control rods were withdrawn, and the power rose again. Everyone breathed a sigh of relief.

They had relaxed too soon.

By 1 a.m. the pressure in the reactor seemed to be steady at 200 megawatts. There were 18 control rods in the reactor.

"If you are finally ready," Dyatlov said sarcastically, "I'd like to start the test."

Toptunov and his foreman, Akimov, remained nervous. The manual said the power level should be 700 megawatts. But no one wanted Dyatlov jumping down his throat, so they kept their mouths shut.

The time had come to test what would happen if the plant should suddenly lose power. One of the engineers shut off the power to the giant turbines. This set off a deadly chain reaction.

The turbines slowed down.

This caused the pumps to push less water into the reactor's core.

Less water caused a hot spot to develop in the bottom of the reactor.

The hot spot turned the remaining water into high-pressure steam.

Suddenly, several loud thuds came from deep inside the building. The door to the control room burst open and a worker ran in, panic written across his face. He had been walking on the catwalk above the reactor. The caps to the fuel channels were jumping up and down in their sockets.

The reactor was going to blow.

Akimov pressed an emergency button to lower all 211 control rods into the reactor's core at once. The pressure should have fallen immediately, but this was where a flaw in the RBMK design became fatal. The control rods had graphite tips. Graphite speeds up nuclear fission. When the rod tips hit the uranium fuel, power surged and the heat inside the core skyrocketed.

The steam could no longer be contained.

At 1:23 a.m., reactor 4 threw off its 1,200-ton cover and blasted 50 tons of nuclear fuel 3,000 feet into the air. Seven hundred tons of radioactive graphite was sprayed throughout the plant.

The control room was plunged into darkness and filled with dust that smelled like the air after a thunderstorm. This was the stench of death—the invisible killer of radiation.

Sasha Yuvchenko was in his office talking to another worker when a tremendous blast blew off the doors of the room. Clouds of dust and steam billowed in.

"What happened?" asked the other man.

"It may be a war," said Yuvchenko.

An exploding reactor was the farthest thing from his mind. "We all thought the safety measures were reliable," he said later. "We believed what we were told in the work manual."

The phone on Yuvchenko's desk rang. The supervisor in the unit for reactor 3 needed a stretcher from the first aid supplies. Yuvchenko grabbed the stretcher and ran.

He had not gone far when he bumped into someone who looked like he'd stepped out of a horror movie. The man's face was covered in blisters and blood. Not until the man spoke did Yuvchenko realize he was one of the water pump operators.

"Help Gena," the man gasped. "He is still by the pumps."

Yuvchenko ran to the pump room. It was dark and looked empty. Then, he saw a man on the ground, filthy and shivering with shock.

Yuvchenko bent to help him, but the man shook his head. "Help Khodemchuk. He's still trapped up there."

Yuvchenko looked in the direction the man pointed. There was nothing there but empty space. Khodemchuk had been blown sky high.

Yuvchenko led the wounded man out of the ruined pump room and ran into the day shift foreman, Yuri Tregub. He should have been home in bed but had stayed past his shift to observe the safety test. Yuvchenko and Tregub went outside to see if they could discover what had caused the explosion.

They exited a side door and found themselves on a road outside the plant. From that position, they had a clear view of the complex.

"What we saw was terrifying," Yuvchenko recalled later. "Everything that could be destroyed, had been." Half of the building for reactor 4 was gone. The entire machine room had vanished, a huge hole in its place. The water coolant system was destroyed. The right side of the reactor hall had collapsed and on the left side, only pipes dangled, like a great beast's wounded limbs quivering in the night sky.

A beam of light shot up from the reactor. It glowed whitish-blue, like a laser. Yuvchenko thought, "It was very beautiful." Fortunately for Yuvchenko, Tregub was older and more experienced—he knew that light was radiation rays.

"We're not sightseeing," Tregub said, and yanked Yuvchenko back into the power station.

On their way to the control room, Yuvchenko and Tregub met three workers headed to the reactor hall. Deputy Chief Engineer Dyatlov had ordered them to lower the 211 control rods into the reactor by hand.

"This is useless," Yuvchenko said as he followed them. "There is no reactor hall anymore and probably no control rods either."

The men climbed 23 floors as water from the ruptured cooling tanks rained down on them. They reached the top level, which was made of reinforced concrete, where they found the massive concrete door had shifted on its hinges. Yuvchenko stood behind the door, holding it open so the other three men could crawl onto the steel rafters and search for the levers that would lower the control rods.

Yuvchenko heard the men gasp. When they looked down through the tangle of steam and concrete, there was no sign of reactor 4. A volcanic crater had taken its place.

By 3 a.m., Yuvchenko began to vomit. By 5 a.m., he could not walk. The radiation levels in the plant were so high, the instruments could not read them. Men were collapsing all over the plant.

Meanwhile, the reactor continued to burn.

———◆———

Lyudmilla Ignatenko and her husband, Vasily, were newlyweds. They lived in the dormitory of the fire station in Pripyat, where Vasily worked. A noise woke Lyudmilla in the middle of the night. She sat up in bed and looked out the window. Vasily was already getting dressed.

"Close the window and go back to sleep," he said. "There's a fire at the reactor. I'll be back soon."

She closed the window, but watched the sky from her bed. "Everything was radiant. The whole sky. A tall flame. And smoke." Hours passed, and her husband never returned.

# Eruptions and Explosions

The first firemen who arrived at the power plant to battle the fire had no protective gear. No one warned them that everything they touched was radioactive. That night, 30 firemen answered the alarm. All of them received lethal doses of radiation, including Vasily Ignatenko.

Radiation comes from elements with unstable atoms. Uranium, the fuel inside reactor 4, is one of these radioactive elements. When a person receives a large dose of radiation during a short period of time, he gets radiation sickness.

How sick a person gets depends on how much radiation their body absorbs.

The first signs of toxic exposure are vomiting, diarrhea, headache, and fever. If a person is lucky, they will not get worse. But if they received a full blast of radiation, symptoms of radiation poisoning appear days or even a few weeks later.

The person bleeds from the nose, mouth, and gums. They suffer from bloody diarrhea. Dizziness and weakness make it hard to function. Their hair falls out. The skin turns red, then blisters and peels off. Sometimes, these radiation burns go all the way to the bone. Wounds do not heal and the body cannot fight off infection.

The invisible cloud rose out of Chernobyl, drifting across acres of forest. Green pines turned red as they were scorched by the toxic wind. Radioactive particles fell in drops of black rain.

Then, the wind shifted direction. The Soviet republics of Ukraine, Belarus, and Russia were in its path. Beyond them lay the rest of Western Europe. Someone had to alert the world of the disaster of Chernobyl.

———◆———

Remember, the Communist Party did not admit mistakes. Soviet leaders, from plant officials to leaders of the Communist Party, covered up the catastrophe.

The plant manager and chief engineer did not inform their superiors in Moscow about the explosion until after 5 a.m. on April 26. Even then, they just said there had been a fire at Chernobyl. No one mentioned an exploded reactor. The Chernobyl officials assured their bosses that everything was under control.

The plant manager accepted the word of the official charged with taking radiation readings at the plant. This man's device showed only a moderate rise in radiation. Some workers frantically argued that these readings could not be correct. Firemen and workers were collapsing.

But the plant manager signed the documents proving to his superiors that everything was fine.

Leaders in Moscow ordered scientific experts sent to Chernobyl. However, until this team arrived, the order was given to say nothing to alarm the people of Pripyat.

Lyudmilla Ignatenko was already alarmed. She received a call at 7 a.m. Her husband had been taken to the hospital. Lyudmilla ran there.

When Vasily saw her, he yelled, "Get out of here! Go!" Lyudmilla was pregnant with their first child and Vasily was afraid he would contaminate his wife and unborn baby.

Lyudmilla headed for home, intending to return later. Military trucks were everywhere in Pripyat. People wondered why the soldiers were wearing surgical masks and washing the streets with some kind of white powder. But the presence of the army calmed people. The government was in charge. Everything would be fine.

Life in Pripyat went on as normal. People bought bread from the bakery. They drank coffee and ate breakfast at outdoor cafes. Children went to school as on any other day.

Of course, rumors were inevitable. As a precaution, teachers kept students inside during recess. When school was dismissed, they told the children to go straight home.

Alesksandr Sirota was 10 years old—he ignored his teacher's order. Alesksandr and his buddies played in the stream and built forts until darkness fell. No one told them the water they were splashing in could kill them.

By early afternoon on April 26, the radiation levels in the town square of Pripyat were 15,000 times the normal amount. Radiation continued to climb all day. Reactor number 4 was still burning.

Finally, on the afternoon of April 27, officials made an announcement to the people of Pripyat. An "unsatisfactory radioactive situation" had occurred at the power station. As a "temporary precaution," Pripyat would be evacuated.

Residents were told they would be gone for only three days. Their possessions would be safe. The town and houses would be cleaned and checked for safety, and then everyone could come back home. Buses ferried citizens out of the city.

They would never return.

# Eruptions and Explosions

It was Sweden, not the Soviet Union, that sounded the international alarm. On April 28, Swedish operators at a monitoring station more than 800 miles from Chernobyl detected radiation levels 40 percent higher than normal. Such high levels indicated a major accident had occurred somewhere in Europe.

Nothing had been reported to officials with the International Atomic Energy Committee.

American spy satellites noticed smoke wafting up from Chernobyl. The director of the International Atomic Energy Committee contacted officials in the Soviet Union. The evening of Monday, April 28, Soviet leaders finally told the world about Chernobyl.

At the bottom of reactor 4, 1,200 tons of white-hot magma continued to burn, sending radioactive dust into the atmosphere. The danger was not over. All of Europe was at the mercy of the wind.

Radioactive rain was reported from France to Corsica and from Great Britain to Greece. In Chernobyl, radiation levels continued to rise. Engineers and physicists feared that if the burning reactor was not extinguished, it could spark an explosion that would ignite the other three reactors in the plant.

Such a disaster would destroy all of Europe.

———◆———

An aerial photo of reactor 4
photo credit: stahlmandesign

Heroic men and women tried multiple strategies to douse reactor 4. Pilots flew over the open roof of the damaged building. They dropped sandbags and boric acid into the reactor. Some pilots made 33 flights in one day, absorbing radiation with each flight.

There was a fear that if uranium leaked through the concrete floor of the reactor into water below it, the water molecules could interact with the uranium and cause another explosion. To try and avoid this scenario, technicians crawled through cable channels and used blow torches to break into reactor 4's building to drain the water.

Thousands of miners dug a 90-foot tunnel and constructed a room large enough to hold a refrigeration device to cool off the reactor. The refrigerator was never set up because on May 10, the fire in reactor 4 suddenly burned out.

The chairman of the government's Chernobyl commission announced, "The main threat from . . . Chernobyl . . . has gone."

The world had dodged a bullet. Now, what remained was to clean up, cover up, and isolate the radiated areas.

Tens of thousands of workers came to Chernobyl. Wearing protective clothing, these men worked one-minute shifts, removing lumps of radioactive graphite from the roof of the reactor 3 building. They bulldozed and buried topsoil. They chopped down pine trees that had turned yellow and red. They dumped contaminated cars and trucks. Hunting squads killed dogs and cats and other animals that could carry contamination into the outside world.

Rural villages were bulldozed until the landscape looked as though they had never existed.

Then reactor 4 was entombed. A giant steel and concrete sarcophagus was constructed over the blown-out reactor. Its deadly remains could not be removed, but officials hoped it could be contained for tens of thousands of years.

◆

The tragedy of Chernobyl is most visible in individual lives. At first, 10-year-old Aleksandr Sirota found the evacuation of Pripyat exciting. But when rumors circulated that no one would be allowed to return, "only there did I first keenly feel the pain of having lost all that was dearest to me: friends, classmates. . . ."

Dreams were all that remained of his childhood.

Sasha Yuvchenko survived, but continues to suffer. Every part of his body that touched debris on the night of the explosion began to burn. Radiation gnawed through one shoulder, his hip, and his calf, turning the skin black and swollen. Bone marrow transfusions and skin grafts saved Yuvchenko's life. He spent one year in the hospital and another two years in rehabilitation.

He avoids talking about Chernobyl because, he says, "There is a stigma attached to it." But he is alive to tell his story.

Vasily Ignatenko was not so lucky. His bone marrow transfusion did not save him. Each time Lyudmilla visited him, Vasily had grown worse. Burns appeared in his mouth and on his tongue and cheeks. His skin turned blue, red, then gray-brown.

Lyudmilla refused to leave his side even though the nurses told her he was a human nuclear reactor.

Lyudmilla said, "I was like a dog, running after them . . . begging and pleading." The nurses pitied her and let her stay with her husband.

But one day, she left Vasily's bedside to attend the funerals of two of the firemen who had worked with her husband. When she returned from the cemetery, she stopped at the nurse's desk.

"How is he?" she asked.

"He died 15 minutes ago," said the nurse.

A few months later, Lyudmilla gave birth to a baby girl. The little girl's liver was contaminated with radiation and she died four hours after birth.

The number of people killed by the Chernobyl explosion is a hotly debated topic. Officially, only two men died in the blast, and another 48 died shortly afterward. The controversy enters the picture when trying to determine how many people were killed by radioactive fallout.

In 1988, the Soviet Union claimed only 31 people had died from radiation and no one would suffer future ill effects. The United Nations predicted 9,000 people would ultimately die from radiation-related illness. The organization Greenpeace estimated the death toll would reach 93,000.

The only area scientists seem to agree on is that children exposed to radiation from Chernobyl have a higher risk of thyroid cancer. Scientists simply do not understand radiation's effects on humans very well. It is hard to prove a direct link to the Chernobyl explosion when cancers and disabilities show up years later.

A 1,000-square-mile exclusion zone encircles the Chernobyl Nuclear Power Plant. The city of Pripyat lies inside this no-man's-land. Walking the streets are the ghosts of the young engineer Leonid Toptunov and his foreman, Alexander Akimov. Both men died from radiation sickness days after the explosion. Vasily Ignatenko's spirit rides the rusty Ferris wheel, his infant daughter in his arms. Living people might return to Pripyat someday. But not for a long, long, time. The environment will not be safe for humans for another 24,000 years.

But all is not dead around Chernobyl. Wolves, black storks, eagles, and a rare breed of horse roam this land. Pine trees have returned to claim their stake in the scorched landscape. The wolves might not live long and the pine trees might be stunted, but still they are there. Nature is resilient in a land that humans almost destroyed.

GEORGIA

ALABAMA

MISSISSIPPI

FLORIDA

LOUISIANA

★

MACONDO WELL
AND
DEEPWATER HORIZON
OIL RIG

OIL SPILL AREA

GULF OF MEXICO

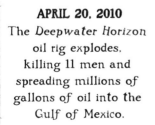

**APRIL 20, 2010**

The *Deepwater Horizon*
oil rig explodes,
killing 11 men and
spreading millions of
gallons of oil into the
Gulf of Mexico.

YOU
ARE
HERE

N
W — E
S

Chapter Five

# Treasure Lost—Blowout on the *Deepwater Horizon*

The Gulf of Mexico is full of treasure. Golden beaches. Underwater cathedrals of coral. Dolphins dancing through the waves. But modern treasure hunters crave a different sort of prize. To find it, they descend to the seafloor, a world of eternal darkness. The hunters burrow deep into the earth's crust, beneath sediment more than 1 million years old. At last, the thick, black treasure comes gushing up—oil.

Drilling for oil in deep water is risky. The British Petroleum oil company gambled and dug 3½ miles into the seafloor of the Gulf of Mexico to locate a huge oil reservoir. Then, the company got lax and greedy and lost its bet.

On April 20, 2010, the drilling rig *Deepwater Horizon* exploded, killing 11 men. Millions of gallons of oil gushed into the sea.

# Eruptions and Explosions

The brown pelican soared over the sea, looking for lunch. Usually, she stayed within a few miles of the Louisiana shore, but today she went much farther.

The *Deepwater Horizon* oil drilling rig floated 48 miles out in the Gulf of Mexico. The pelican soared over the 378-foot-tall vessel that had a deck as big as a football field. A 25-story derrick dominated the deck. This steel tower held the drill and pipes used to dig deep into the sea bed. Two huge industrial cranes flanked the derrick. The pelican spotted a school of mullet fish. Forgetting about the strange rig below, she followed her lunch.

The 125 men and one woman on *Deepwater Horizon* ignored the pelican. They lived in the middle of nature, but their jobs depended on the world of modern technology.

Some experts estimate the Gulf holds as much as 45 billion barrels of crude oil, and oil companies have been drilling in its deep waters since the 1990s. British Petroleum has been in business since 1903, but its safety record in the twenty-first century was stained. Fatal accidents occurred at BP facilities in 2005 and 2007, and the company racked up hundreds of safety violations.

Despite this record, in 2009 the U.S. government leased BP a section of seafloor in the Gulf called the Macondo Prospect. Exploratory studies showed large oil and natural gas deposits lay underground.

From the start, the project ran into trouble.

◆

BP hired another company, called Transocean, to drill a well into Macondo. Transocean started the job in the fall of 2009, but a hurricane damaged its rig, so the company replaced it with *Deepwater Horizon*. To understand what went wrong with *Deepwater Horizon* on April 20, 2010, we need some background knowledge.

Drilling rigs dig blindly into sand and bedrock at the bottom of the sea, a landscape full of canyons and ridges. Once part of the well hole is drilled, the crew inserts sections of pipe casing into it. Casing keeps the well from collapsing and keeps contaminants from coming up the well pipe to the surface.

The contaminant that worries crews most is gas. Pockets of methane under the sea bed can build up pressure. Little gas bubbles try to sneak into the well pipe. To keep gas out, crews push cement between the bedrock wall and the outside of the well pipe. The cement hardens. Gaps between casing sections seal, keeping gas bubbles out.

This cement is not the stuff used on city sidewalks. It must be able to stand up to cold temperatures on the ocean floor, boiling hot oil, and intense pressure.

Oil drilling operations need mud, although not the kind found in puddles on a rainy day. Oil drilling mud resembles a chocolate milkshake. Made from a combination of water and clay, oil drilling mud is pumped down the drill hole to prevent the walls from caving in. It also lubricates and cools the drill bit as it grinds through bedrock.

The pressure of mud in the well acts like a finger held over a fizzing soda bottle to prevent oil and gas from shooting up the hole.

The drilling rig's final task is to plug the well. One plug is placed at the bottom of the well where it opens into the oil reservoir. Seawater is pumped into the well pipe and a second plug seals the top of the well on the seafloor. The actual pumping of oil up to the surface is done later by a production crew.

The accident every drilling crew fears is a blowout. This occurs when gas and oil erupt uncontrollably from the well, poisoning the water for miles around. If a spark is ignited during a blowout, the entire rig could explode.

To prevent blowouts, crews rely on a 50-foot-tall stack of valves called the blowout preventer, or BOP.

The BOP sits on the ocean floor and is connected to the well pipe. In an emergency, the crew activates a pair of clamps to close off the connection between the well and the rig. The BOP is the final tool every crew relies on to prevent disasters.

The BOP on *Deepwater Horizon* was 10 years old. It had lots of problems that the crew overlooked or ignored. It was also long overdue for a safety inspection.

The brown pelican positioned herself for the kill. With wings spread, she drifted on the wind and aimed her massive beak at the water like a heat-seeking missile. Then, from a height of 60 feet, she plunged headfirst into the sea. Underwater, the bird's throat pouch swelled, trapping a mouthful of fish and a couple gallons of water. She returned to the surface and tipped her head back and swallowed her lunch. Life was good on the Gulf.

The crew on the *Deepwater Horizon* might have envied the pelican her carefree life. Its 126 people labored long hours. Some worked for Transocean and others for BP. The day was divided into two 12-hour shifts. Crews remained on the rig for three weeks and then received three weeks of shore leave.

# Eruptions and Explosions

Despite the grueling schedule, the pay was good and the crew became a family. Sundays meant barbeques on the deck. In the evening, people enjoyed stunning sunsets and card games with friends. But the dangers of the job were never far from their minds.

When Mike Williams came aboard *Deepwater Horizon* as chief electronics technician in 2009, he spotted problems. His job was to maintain the fire and gas detection and alarm systems. These systems were a mess.

The rig's general alarm system had been silenced. If sensors detected a life-threatening situation, no sirens would sound. Williams was told that false alarms woke people up in the middle of the night too often. Williams's bosses told him watchers on the bridge could keep an eye on sensors. In a real emergency, they would trigger a general alarm. But Williams knew in a crisis, every second mattered.

What mattered most to BP executives was finishing the drilling of the Macondo well. The project was behind schedule and over budget.

The Macondo well liked to "kick." When small pockets of gas inside the earth rise, they expand. A few cubic feet of underground gas could fill a sports stadium on the surface. Sometimes, gas unexpectedly flowed into the well and kicked seawater and mud back up the hole.

Jason Anderson was an expert on controlling these kicks. He had worked on *Deepwater Horizon* since it first launched in 2001 and could recognize clues about what was happening at the bottom of the well. For example, the amount of mud coming back up the well had to match the amount that was pumped into it. Too much mud coming up meant gas down below was kicking it. Too little mud coming up meant there were cracks in the bottom of the well leaking mud.

Macondo kicked and leaked and both problems cost time and money. Every barrel of mud that escaped through a crack in the well cost BP hundreds of dollars. Drilling had to stop while the operators pumped a plaster made of ground-up peanut and walnut shells into the well to plug the leaks.

The crew nicknamed Macondo the "well from hell."

Every delay made the BP company men more anxious. On his last home leave, Jason Anderson complained to his father about the way BP was running things to make up for time lost to delays. Pressure to drill faster. Constantly changing plans. Orders to cut corners. This made dangerous work more dangerous.

But Anderson's time on *Deepwater Horizon* was almost over. He had been promoted and was supposed to start work on another rig on April 14.

His bosses begged Anderson to stay on for just one more week. He agreed, and a helicopter was scheduled to pick him up from the rig on April 21.

The male pelican swaggered down the beach like a cowboy who had been in the saddle too long. The female pelican liked the look of him. Instinct told her the time had come to settle down. The male bird began to flirt in the pelican way, dipping and swaying from side to side. It worked. The birds flew off into the sunset together. But their happily ever after would not last long.

On April 9, BP decided *Deepwater Horizon* had drilled deep enough—13,293 feet below the sea bed. Now, the crew only had to cement the top and bottom of the well hole and their job would be done.

The cement mixture was critical at this point. If the well bottom was in loose rock and sand, cement might ooze into this soft stuff and fail to form a solid-enough barrier to keep the oil and gas out of the well. BP engineers in Houston, Texas, spent five days troubleshooting which cement mix to use, then relayed their decision to BP's top man on the rig.

Jimmy Harrell was the Transocean employee in charge of drilling on *Deepwater Horizon*. He had worked on oil rigs for 30 years and it took a lot to shock him. The morning of April 19, when the BP man ordered Harrell to use cement with added nitrogen to seal the well, Harrell was shocked.

Nitrogen makes the cement foam. Like shaving cream in the bottom of a sink, it tends to stay in place rather than seep through a crack. Harrell used foam cement often, but not 2 miles into the earth. Foam cement was usually used just below the muddy ocean floor. The deeper the cement was pumped, the more intense the pressure grew. Harrell was concerned that high pressure would squeeze the nitrogen bubbles out of the cement and up into the well pipe, creating channels for gas and oil to follow.

Harrell argued, but the BP boss refused to budge and the foam cement was poured.

The pelican pair built their nest on a barrier island off the coast of Louisiana. The female rested her webbed feet on the eggs to keep them warm. She watched waves crash on the shore while her mate soared overhead looking for fish. The Gulf was peaceful, the perfect place to bring chicks into the world. Far out in the distance, the pelican saw a tiny speck—*Deepwater Horizon*.

The morning of April 20, the crew of *Deepwater Horizon* had to perform one final test before they could plug the top of the well and pack up and go home. In what was called the "negative test," the crew removed all the heavy mud from the well, replacing it with lighter seawater. Then, they shut the well and waited to see if pressure built up in the well pipe. If it did, that meant gas and oil were seeping into the well.

This was a complicated test that took a long time. Plus, its results were open to interpretation. One of the BP officials on board wanted to skip the negative test, but Jimmy Harrell dug in his heels. "Skipping the negative test is not my policy," he told the man.

This time, the BP man backed down.

As the negative test got underway, a helicopter delivered four businessmen from Transocean and BP to *Deepwater Horizon*. These executives had arrived to present the crew with a safety award. In the last seven years, the *Deepwater Horizon* had not had any accidents that lost production time. Everyone knew time was money.

As the VIPs toured the rig, operators removed the mud in the well pipe little by little. If the cement had done its job, the pressure gauges should drop to zero as the heavy mud was removed.

That did not happen.

Several pipes connected to the main well pipe. One of these was called the kill line. While the pressure in the kill line dropped to zero, the main drill pipe still showed 1,250 pounds of pressure per square inch. The crew was confused. They decided to repeat the test.

At 6 p.m., the shift changed and new men took over the test. BP's nightshift man was convinced the pressure reading on the kill line was accurate, and he gave the order to remove the rest of the mud in the drill line and cap the well.

Some crew members wondered if the foam cement in the bottom of the well had hardened yet. Usually, a cement bonding test is performed. But that meant more time and more money.

BP officials decided to skip this test.

At 8 p.m., the sun dropped below the horizon and the sky turned brilliant shades of pink, orange, and red. Two crew members sat in the cabs of their cranes, 185 feet above the water, enjoying the view.

Jason Anderson was working the night shift in the drill shack. His friend and senior toolpusher, Randy Ezell, offered to stick around and help withdraw the mud. "Man, you ain't got to do that," Anderson said. "I've got this. If I have any problem at all . . . I'll give you a call." Ezell had been on duty for 12 hours and was exhausted. He left Anderson to do the job.

Ezell would never see his friend again

For an hour, the operators withdrew mud. The storage tanks could not hold all of it, so from 9:15 to 9:30, the men were busy pumping 400 barrels overboard. During this time, no one noticed the pressure gauge on the drill pipe steadily rise.

Deep down below the seafloor, a fountain of methane gas entered the drill pipe through the weak cement. It shot upward, gaining speed. The gas shoved mud and water ahead of it, faster and faster. Up on the rig, mud began to spill onto the drilling room floor.

The time was 9:38. Deep below the waves, the gas reached the BOP where it perched on the ocean floor. The BOP could have wrapped a stranglehold around the drill pipe and cut off the gas and its race to the surface. But no one activated it. Once the gas sailed past the BOP, there was no stopping it.

Jason Anderson suddenly realized something was wrong. He could feel the well boiling. At 9:42, he activated the BOP. It was too late. Mud and gas exploded out of the top of the derrick and surges of gas whooshed loudly.

Anderson yelled to his assistant driller. "Call Randy."

A crack appeared on one of the eggs in the pelicans' nest. It shot through the egg and a chip of shell broke off. A grayish-pink, hairless baby pelican poked its beak out of the hole. The chick's eyes were shut tight and it grunted as it wriggled into the world. The other chicks followed. The mother and father bird perched close by, prepared to keep their babies safe from harm.

These birds were powerless to safeguard their young from the danger that loomed on *Deepwater Horizon*.

A volcano of mud and water erupted from the derrick. Inside the engine room, more mud and water slammed around the room. The engines whined and howled.

The two crane operators who had been enjoying the sunset now saw a smoky haze of gas waft out of a pipe high on the derrick. The mist fell over the deck and slipped into the air vents that led into the engine room.

On the bridge, the captain and his mates were showing off the rig's state-of-the-art control room to the VIPs. Captain Curt Kuchta and bridge officer Andrea Fleytas heard a loud hissing.

Camera monitors showed mud flying into the sea. Gas sensors lit up alarm buttons and another monitor showed the cloud of gas spreading over the rig. *Deepwater Horizon* was a ticking time bomb just waiting for a spark.

The general alarm that Mike Williams had worried about months ago was still on silent mode.

Engine number three exploded first, quickly followed by engine six. The ship lost power. Now, there was no way to disconnect the rig from the well pipe, where an unending supply of gas and oil surged toward the surface.

Randy Ezell had been dozing in his room below deck when the call came from the drilling room. He raced into the toolpusher's office to grab his hardhat. Suddenly, the lights went out and a massive explosion hurled him into a wall 20 feet away.

Ezell blinked and tried to clear his head. He lay on his back covered in debris. Ezell tried to rise, but his legs were trapped. He tried again and still could not get free. Panic surged through him, but Ezell fought it. "Either you get up or you're going to lay here and die," he told himself.

Heaving with all his might, Ezell managed to slide his legs out from under the pile of wood and metal.

Smoke filled the room, so Ezell stayed close to the floor, where the air was a bit fresher. As he crawled into the hallway, he touched something soft. A body.

A flashlight flickered and a minute later, two other crew members joined Ezell. The beam of the flashlight revealed the identity of the man on the floor: toolpusher Wyman Wheeler. He was buried under a huge pile of debris, but he was still alive. The men uncovered him and tried to pick him up, but Wheeler howled in pain.

The men heard someone else moaning. "God help me. Somebody please help me." The voice was coming from an office door, where only a pair of feet stuck out from under a pile of debris. Ezell and the other men dug out Buddy Trahan, one of the VIP officials who had arrived just that day. Trahan's neck had a golf-ball size hole in it, his back was charred from neck to belt, and bone peeked through a long gash on his thigh.

With the aid of a stretcher, the five men made it to the deck and headed for the lifeboat station.

Mike Williams was in the electronic technician's shop talking to his wife on the phone when he heard a hissing noise and a thump. Williams's office was next door to the engine control room.

# Eruptions and Explosions

Through the air vents that ran between rooms, Williams heard a beeping alarm. The engine control room held the six large diesel engines that powered the rig.

He said goodbye to his wife and started to stand up when the computer monitor exploded in his face. The lights overhead shattered, raining shards of glass. Williams found his way to the door and had just put his hand on the door handle when a tremendous bang yanked the door off its hinges and slammed it into Williams's forehead.

When Williams regained consciousness, he was pressed up against a wall with the door on top of him. "This is it. I am going to die right here," he thought.

The room filled with smoke and Williams could barely breathe. Blood dripped down his forehead and into his eyes, blinding him. He dropped to his hands and knees and crawled down the hallway to the next door. This door exploded too, throwing him 35 feet backward. Now, Williams was angry. Fire doors were meant to protect the crew, but "these fire doors were trying to kill me," Williams later said in an interview.

Williams refused to let them. One shoulder and one leg did not move properly, but he managed to crawl down the hallway toward a light, where he found other men. They helped each other climb to the main deck.

Where the derrick should have been, they found a tower of flames shooting 200 feet into the sky.

The deck was covered in mud. Cracks and pops rippled through the air as fire spread. Panic spread, too. Everyone ran for the lifeboats.

One crew member repeatedly pushed the button that would sever the tether connecting *Deepwater Horizon* to the well. But without power, the emergency disconnect would not work. Captain Kuchta gave the order to abandon ship.

Heat baked the lifeboat deck. As people crawled into the enclosed boats, the vessels filled with smoke. The flaming derrick hurled fireballs at the lifeboat deck. Even though all crew members were not accounted for, the boats were launched.

When Randy Ezell finally made it to the deck with Wyman Wheeler on the stretcher, the lifeboats were gone. Several other people were still on deck.

"We're taking the life rafts," Captain Kuchta said. As they inflated a 20-foot plastic life raft, the crew could feel and smell their hair singe from nearby flames. Wyman Wheeler screamed in pain as his stretcher was shoved on board. Two explosions followed in rapid succession.

Someone released the lever holding the raft to the
rig. It rocked forward and plunged 50 feet into the
water, tipping as it fell. People inside tumbled around,
and Andrea Fleytas, the only female crew member,
fell out the open door. Her head popped up from
the oily water. The raft was right beside her and she
clung to it.

Below the rig, the water was in flames.

Mike Williams and two other men watched the
life raft fall into the sea. Two life rafts remained on
the rig, but three men could not deploy them quickly
enough. The fire was going to devour them any
second.

"We can stay here and die," Williams said, "or we
can jump." One man leaped and the second man
followed. Williams said a prayer and jumped.

The plunge into the sea felt like an eternity.
Williams kicked furiously and finally broke the
surface. He inhaled a huge breath and immediately
his skin and eyes began to burn. Diesel fuel floated
over the surface of the water and fire skated across
the waves only a few yards away. Williams swam in
the opposite direction.

photo credit: U.S. Coast Guard

He felt as though he swam for hours. The pain in his head disappeared and he wondered if he was dead. Then, a strong pair of hands appeared from nowhere and hauled Williams onto a rescue boat.

The crew of a nearby ship pulled almost two dozen survivors out of the sea that night. Ninety-four people escaped on the lifeboats and made it to the rescue ship. When one of the *Deepwater Horizon* crew took roll call, 11 men were missing—all had been on duty on the rig floor when the engines exploded. Coast guard helicopters and rescue boats searched, but the bodies of these 11 men were never found.

Jason Anderson's last day of work on *Deepwater Horizon* was also his last day of life.

◆

# Eruptions and Explosions

On April 22, *Deepwater Horizon* tipped over and sank, causing a second catastrophe. As the rig plunged to the seafloor, the drill pipe broke. Crude oil spewed into the Gulf at a rate of 2½ million gallons a day. BP tried to seal the well, but failed again and again. The water in the Gulf of Mexico turned from blue to brown as oil gushed for 87 days.

The Macondo well was not permanently sealed until September 18.

This was the worst oil spill in U.S. history. More than 200 million gallons of crude oil polluted the Gulf, devastating the economy of the Gulf States. Tar balls ruined the beaches. Crab fishermen found their crates empty. No one wanted to eat Gulf shrimp. Shrimpers, bait shops, restaurants, and many others went out of business.

An oil slick in the Gulf
photo credit: Petty Officer 1st Class Michael B. Watkins

The mother pelican did not mean to kill her children. The father bird guarded the nest while she went fishing. From high above the ocean, her keen eyes spotted a dark plume drifting through the water below. She dove, emerging moments later with a pouch full of mullet fish and oily water.

The flight back to the nest was exhausting. Greasy, black oil dripped from the pelican's wings, weighing her down. Back at the nest, the pelican opened her beak. Three hungry chicks dipped their beaks in and gulped down their lunch.

While the chicks filled their bellies with toxins, the father pelican tried to clean his own oily feathers. Each time he rubbed his beak over his body, he ate more poison. The chicks and their father were soon dead.

The female pelican sat forlornly on her now empty nest. Oil seeped through her feathers into her skin and tar slathered her once grand beak.

Brown pelicans were not *Deepwater Horizon*'s only victims. Dolphins, sea turtles, spotted trout, tuna, red snapper, sperm whales, and coral are dying at higher rates and reproducing at lower rates since the oil spill. Greed and the world's addiction to an oily treasure damaged the true treasures of the Gulf for decades to come.

**acidic:** from acids, which are chemical compounds that taste sour, bitter, or tart. Examples are vinegar and lemon juice. Water also contains some acid.

**aerosol:** a substance contained under pressure and released by a gas as a spray.

**alliance:** a formal agreement between nations to help each other.

**Allies:** an alliance between France, England, the Soviet Union, and the United States during World War II.

**almanac:** a reference book containing weather forecasts, lists and tables, moon phases, and tide charts.

**archipelago:** a group of islands, usually arranged in a line near a bigger piece of land.

**atmosphere:** a layer of gas surrounding the earth.

**atom:** a tiny particle of matter.

**atomic:** energy that comes from an atom.

**Axis powers:** an alliance between Germany, Italy, and Japan during World War II.

**bankrupt:** to be unable to repay debts.

**Big Six:** the Japanese council that controlled how World War II was fought.

**blowout preventer:** a device used by oil drilling crews in an emergency to close off an oil well.

**blowout:** when gas and oil erupt uncontrollably from a well.

**bludgeon:** a short stick used as a weapon.

**boiler:** a tank that generates high-pressure steam.

**bombardier:** the crew member responsible for sighting and releasing bombs.

**bribe:** to give someone money so they will do something illegal or dishonest for you.

**bumper crop:** a very big crop.

**cabinet:** a body of advisers.

**cataclysmic:** a violent natural event.

**catastrophe:** a sudden event that causes great damage or suffering.

**circumnavigate:** to go all the way around.

**Civil War:** a war between the Northern and Southern states in the United States that lasted from 1861 to 1865.

**civilian:** a member of society who is not in the military.

**climate:** the average weather patterns in an area during a long period of time.

**climate change:** changes to the average weather patterns in an area during a long period of time.

**combust:** to consume by fire.

**communism:** a system of government in which the state controls all the land and business and in theory divides the country's wealth evenly between all citizens and all cities.

**Confederate:** a supporter of the Confederate States of America, the rebel nation formed by 11 Southern states that separated from the United States on the eve of the Civil War.

**consciousness:** perceiving or noticing with controlled thought and observation.

**contaminant:** something that makes a substance impure.

**contaminate:** to make impure or dirty by contact or mixture with another substance.

**corpse:** a dead body.

**credit:** the ability of a customer to borrow money on the promise to pay it back later, with an extra charge tacked on called interest.

**crop:** a plant grown for food or other uses.

**crude oil:** oil in its natural form, right out of the ground.

**curdle:** when a substance goes bad and becomes rotten.

**current:** the steady flow of water or air in one direction.

**debris:** scattered pieces of something wrecked or destroyed.

**decapitate:** to have one's head cut off.

**decimate:** to kill, destroy, or remove a large percentage or part of something.

**democracy:** a form of government in which people exercise power through voting.

**desolate:** an empty place with no people.

**detonate:** to explode.

**diplomat:** a person who represents one country to another.

**disembowel:** to have one's guts ripped out.

**dormant:** to be in a resting and inactive state.

**drilling rig:** a large structure with equipment for drilling an oil well.

**drought:** a long period of time with little or no rain.

**dynasty:** a series of rulers who come from the same family.

**economic depression:** a time when the economy struggles and many people lose their jobs.

**economy:** the wealth and resources of a country.

**edible:** safe to eat.

**element:** a substance that cannot be broken down by chemical means; matter is made up of different elements.

**ember:** a glowing, hot coal.

**engineer:** a person who uses science, math, and creativity to design and build things.

**enterprise:** a project or undertaking.

**equator:** the imaginary line around the planet halfway between the North and South Poles.

**erupt:** to burst out suddenly, such as in a volcano.

**eternal:** lasts forever.

**evacuate:** to leave a dangerous place to go to a safe place.

**exclude:** to keep out.

**fallout:** radioactive particles that fall in dust or rain after a nuclear explosion.

**famine:** a period of great hunger and lack of food for a large population.

**fascism:** a form of government that considers the nation more important than the individual and maintains total control over its citizens' lives.

**fertile:** land that is good for growing crops.

**folly:** foolishness or lack of good sense.

**front:** the dividing point where two sides meet.

**gale:** a very strong wind.

**glacier:** a large river of ice that moves down a mountain slope.

**global:** all over the world.

**graphite:** a soft, gray mineral that is used in pencils and also in nuclear reactors.

**hardliner:** someone who sticks to one idea and refuses to compromise.

**harvest:** the process or period of gathering in crops.

**hypothermia:** when the temperature inside the body is too cold.

**immigrate:** to move to a foreign country to live there permanently.

**import:** products or resources brought into a country.

**interest:** the cost a bank charges a customer who borrows money.

**investment:** a purchase made by a person in hopes of a larger future return.

**jet stream:** a high-speed flow of air high in the atmosphere that flows from west to east.

**lava:** hot, melted rock that has risen to the surface of the earth.

**Little Boy:** the atomic bomb dropped on Hiroshima, Japan, on August 6, 1945.

**lubricate:** to apply grease or another substance that allows something to move freely.

**magma:** hot liquid rock below the surface of the earth.

**Manhattan Project:** the United States' secret atomic bomb development program.

**manipulation:** cleverly and unfairly controlling or influencing a person or situation.

**maritime:** having to do with the sea and sailing.

**mediate:** to help two conflicting sides reach an agreement.

**megawatt:** a unit of power.

**meteorologist:** a scientist who studies weather and climate.

**migration:** the movement of a large group of animals or people from one location to another.

**mineral:** a naturally occurring solid found in rocks and in the ground. Rocks are made of minerals. Gold and diamonds are precious minerals.

**moderate:** not extreme.

**mud:** a combination of water and clay pumped into oil wells while they are being drilled to lubricate the drill and to maintain pressure on oil and gas below so they do not surge up the pipe.

**napalm:** a flammable sticky jelly used in firebombs.

**Nazi Party:** the political party led by Adolf Hitler that ruled Germany from 1933 until 1945.

**neutral:** not taking sides during a debate or conflict.

**neutron:** a particle inside the nucleus of an atom.

**nuclear fission:** a chain reaction in which the nucleus of an atom splits and releases energy.

**nuclear:** energy produced when the nucleus of an atom is split apart.

**nucleus:** the core of an atom. Plural is nuclei.

**patriotism:** love of one's country.

**perpetual:** never ending or changing.

**plains:** large, flat areas of land.

# Glossary

**Potsdam Declaration:** the terms for Japan's surrender in World War II.

**prime minister:** the head of a government.

**profitable:** describes a business or activity that makes money.

**province:** a region of a country.

**pumice:** a light rock full of air spaces, formed from solidified lava.

**pyroclastic flow:** the current of lava and dirt that spreads out along the ground from a volcano after an eruption.

**radiation:** energy rays that come from nuclear energy.

**raja:** a native ruler of small kingdoms of Indonesian islands during the nineteenth century.

**reactor:** a device designed to maintain a chain reaction within the nuclei of atoms in order to create energy, usually to produce electricity.

**republic:** a territorial unit like a state or province.

**revenge:** to hurt someone in exchange for an injury or wrong done to you.

**run amuck:** to behave in a wild, out-of-control manner.

**salvation:** saved or delivered from danger or difficulty.

**sarcophagus:** a tomb.

**scavenge:** to find usable bits and parts from discarded stuff.

**sediment:** dirt, fertilizer, rocks, and other tiny bits of matter deposited in rivers and oceans.

**shock wave:** a sharp change of pressure traveling through air caused by an explosion that moves faster than the speed of sound.

**solar:** relating to the sun.

**soup kitchen:** a place where free food is served to the poor.

**state of the art:** the most recent stage in the development of a product, using the newest ideas and the most up-to-date features.

**steamboat:** a boat with large paddle wheels propelled by a steam-powered engine.

**strait:** a narrow passage of water that connects two larger bodies of water.

**strategist:** someone who plans.

**stratosphere:** the upper region of the atmosphere.

**stunted:** prevented from growing properly.

**sulfur dioxide:** a colorless gas or liquid that adds to air pollution and acid rain.

**summit:** the highest point of a hill or mountain.

**technology:** the tools, methods, and systems used to solve a problem or do work.

**toil:** to work.

**toolpusher:** a person who directs drilling on an oil rig.

**torrent:** a sudden, violent outpouring.

**traitor:** someone who betrays his country.

**transform:** to change dramatically.

**tsunami:** a series of giant waves caused by earthquakes, explosions, meteors, or landslides.

**turbine:** a machine that produces continual power because a wheel is turned by fast-moving water or steam pressure.

**ultimatum:** a final demand.

**unconditional surrender:** a surrender in which no guarantees are given to the losing side.

**universe:** everything that exists, everywhere.

**uranium:** a naturally radioactive chemical element.

**vagabond:** a person who wanders from place to place without a home or job.

**vermin:** small animals or insects that are pests, such as cockroaches or mice.

**villa:** a large country home.

**volcano:** an opening in the earth's surface through which magma, ash, and gases can burst out.

**warlord:** an aggressive military leader with control in government.

**water vapor:** water as a gas, such as steam, mist, or fog.

**wrath:** extreme anger.

# Resources

## Websites

This *National Geographic* site includes articles, maps, and photographs about the Indonesian volcanoes. *ngm.nationalgeographic.com/2008/01/volcano-culture/ andrew-marshall-text*

The Smithsonian Institute has a website with data all about Tambora. *volcano.si.edu/volcano.cfm?vn=264040*

This PBS site examines whether the *Sultana* explosion was caused by Confederate sabotage. *pbs.org/opb/historydetectives/investigation/civil-war-sabotage*

This interactive website by Annenberg Learner lets the viewer weigh in on whether President Truman made the right decision by dropping two atomic bombs on Japan. *learner.org/series/biographyofamerica/prog23/feature/index.html*

## Museums

Trace the path of the *Deepwater Horizon* oil spill on this Smithsonian National Museum of Natural History tool, "Gulf of Mexico Oil Spill Interactive." *ocean.si.edu/gulf-mexico-oil-spill-interactive*

## Videos

Explore more of the effects of Mount Tambora in this video. *youtube.com/watch?v=_2BmIhxfl_I*

Watch a video explaining the *Deepwater Horizon* explosion. *youtube.com/watch?v=N4WtlbeYsoQ*